DARK PSYCHOLOGY

How to analyze people and their body language with dark psychology secrets.

Learn to Identify and Protect Yourself from Harmful People

Bob Brown

© **Copyright 2020 - All rights reserved.**

The content contained within this book may not be reproduced, duplicated, or transmitted without direct written permission from the author or the publisher.

Under no circumstances will any blame or legal responsibility be held against the publisher, or author, for any damages, reparation, or monetary loss due to the information contained within this book. Either directly or indirectly.

Legal Notice:

This book is copyright protected. This book is only for personal use. You cannot amend, distribute, sell, use quote or paraphrase any part, or the content within this book, without the consent of the author or publisher.

Disclaimer Notice:

Please note the information contained within this document is for educational and entertainment purposes only. All effort has been executed to present accurate, up to date, and reliable, complete information. No warranties of any kind are declared or implied.

Readers acknowledge that the author is not engaging in the rendering of legal, financial, medical, or professional advice. The content within this book has been derived from various sources. Please consult a licensed professional before attempting any techniques outlined in this book.

By reading this document, the reader agrees that under no circumstances is the author responsible for any losses, direct or indirect, which are incurred as a result of the use of information contained within this document, including, but not limited to, — errors, omissions, or inaccuracies.

Table of Contents

Introduction..1

Chapter 1..7
- ❖ Perceiving People

Chapter 2..20
- ❖ Understanding Archetypes

Chapter 3..44
- ❖ Analyzing Cognitive Functions

Chapter 4..72
- ❖ Constructing from the Elements

Chapter 5..90
- ❖ The River is never the Same Twice

Chapter 6..102
- ❖ Psychic Prejudice

Chapter 7..118
- ❖ Cold Readings

Chapter 8..134
- ❖ Body Language

Chapter 9..148
- ❖ Detecting Specific Personality Traits through Body Language

Chapter 10...160
- ❖ Detecting Lies

Chapter 11...170
- ❖ Incompatibility.

Chapter12 182
- ❖ Listening to Hear

Conclusion..194

❖ Introduction

How to Analyze People: Dark Psychology Secrets will prepare you to be aware of your own intention, and teach you how to navigate the intentions of others. This will serve as a guide to effective and informed communication.

There is no perfect system to categorize people, but the work of Carl Yung revealed certain habits within humanity. These habits are our reliance on Thought, Feeling, Intuition, and Sensation. Every human displays these attributes, and most can be observed falling within an archetype, such as ENTJ.

ENTJ means Extroverted Intuitive Thinking Judger, which is the archetype that relies on Extroverted Thinking as its primary function, and on Introverted Intuition as its auxiliary type. ISFP means Introverted Sensory Feeling Perceiver. This is the archetype with Introverted Feeling as their primary function and Extroverted Sensation as their auxiliary function. Each type has its own functions, which are sorted according to the same logic.

Learning to read these attitudes will prove to be a great skill for those that quickly want to read others. It allows you to get along with people you might not naturally click with, and to richen the relationships in your life that you have with the people you wish you could understand better.

Below we will continue to discuss the archetypes and how they manifest themselves in the people around us. The system will be

explained further in the text as it goes into the technical aspects, but for the beginning, the shorthand for the archetypes will be used.

❖ Chapter 1 Perceiving People

Everyone has their own habits and peculiarities. It's too tiring to be unique every day of your life because there are simply too

many responsibilities. Without a schedule, life would be chaos. Over time certain strategies rise, and others fall away. Each will have their own experience with this journey, but there are larger patterns within the human story.

Introversion and extroversion are attributes that people are quick to judge in one another. People often perceive themselves as social, or as someone who isn't interested in outings as much as they are in their hobbies. This speaks to natural division within humanity, as people simply have preferences for different things.

Some people are introverted, others are extroverted, and most of us are ambiverts. This means that most of us are somewhere in- between, displaying both introverted and extroverted qualities. The population of people who are only socially focused, and those who are only focused on their own pursuits, is incredibly low compared to the people who are a mix.

Understanding this, the label introvert and extrovert take on a different meaning. When you mention an extrovert you don't mean somebody who only exists in a social capacity, you mean an ambivert with an extroverted leaning. This is a distinction that's important to make because it highlights that a person is not a slave to their type, but an expression of their type. When someone is an introvert that engages in extroverted behavior that does not mean that they are acting out of character. Most people have the capacity for both introverted and extroverted interaction with the world around

them. Almost everybody will have to rely on both introverted and extroverted skills to succeed in life.

However, it can be observed that there are massive gaps in the way that people communicate with one another. Some people are prone to rely on empathy; other people want to rely on the power of their emotions. Even between two emotional people, there are often differences in how those emotions are expressed. Then there are people who prefer to keep things physical, people who are more prone to dialogue. All sorts of people have their own different ways of communicating, but there are common threads between them.

Carl Yung described eight cognitive functions. These functions are Introverted Thinking, Extroverted Thinking, Introverted Feeling, Extroverted Feeling, Introverted Sensation, Extroverted Sensation, Introverted Intuition, and Extroverted Intuition. Everyone has each of these individual functions with them but in a hierarchy. If someone has Introverted Sensing as their primary function, then Introverted Intuition is their weakest function. Each of the functions and their placements determines the mechanics of the different archetypes.

The placement of the four main functions of the personality is the area of focus for this work as the shadow functions are more important when studying therapy than how to analyze others through a social atmosphere. Each archetype has a primary function, an auxiliary function, a tertiary function, and an inferior function. The placements of the functions are such that the primary and the inferior are opposites, as are the auxiliary and tertiary functions. If an individual has Extroverted Intuition primary function, then they will have an Introverted Sensing as an inferior function.

The functions that dominate conversation mostly come down to Introverted Feeling, Extroverted Feeling, Introverted Thinking, and Extroverted Thinking. These are the rational functions or judging functions. They are the functions that allow individuals to organize the world around them and to judge the merit of the world themselves. If an individual has Introverted Feeling as a primary or auxiliary function, then that person has Extroverted Thinking as a tertiary or inferior function. If they have Extroverted Feeling as a primary or auxiliary function, then they have Introverted Thinking as a tertiary or inferior function.

The shorthand names used for the archetypes should be decoded instead of seen as several binaries. An INFJ isn't an introvert as discussed above; they're ambiverts except for a few select purists. Instead of interpreting an INFJ as an introverted Feeler who trusts their intuition one should read the functions that make up the archetype. All judgers have an extroverted judging function; all perceivers have an extroverted perceiving function.

As the INFJ is a judger with feeling for their rational function, their judging function is Extroverted Feeling, but because they're introverted, it's their auxiliary function. Now as their rational function is known their perceiving function needs to be decoded. They're an intuitive archetype, and they're introverted, so that means their primary function will be Introverted Intuition.

Once the primary and auxiliary functions are known, it is easy to find the tertiary and inferior functions. The tertiary function is the opposite of the auxiliary function, and the inferior function is the opposite of the primary function. So, for the INFJ this means that their tertiary function is Introverted Thinking, as their auxiliary function is Extroverted Feeling. Their inferior function is Extroverted Sensation, as Introverted Intuition is their primary function. All of the types can be decoded in this way, and that is what should be understood by the shorthand INFJ. It should not be taken to mean an Introverted Intuitive Feeling Judger, as that does not adequately describe an INFJ.

INFJs can be incredibly cold and calculating people who demand on logic over feelings. This is because they have either underdeveloped their Extroverted Feeling, or they can get caught in a feedback loop between Introverted Intuition and Introverted Thinking. Even though their primary extroverted function is a feeling function, that doesn't mean that they have a healthy relationship with it. The binary falls apart because the ways that people utilize their different functions has endless variety.

For another example, INTPs can be utterly opposed to novelty. ENTPs and INTPs are supposed to be hungry for advancement and new ideas due to the pairing of Extroverted Intuition with Introverted Thinking, but when an INTP gets scared of the world, they can leave their Extroverted Intuition underdeveloped while over-relying on Introverted Sensation. People do not need to act like their archetype to belong to them; this is a system to make sense of humanity, not a code of law.

Once this is understood then basic misconceptions can be done away with, like that Thinkers only get along with Thinkers, or that Feelers only get along with Feelers. The important part of the theory is not where someone fits on binary, but how well they balance the abilities that they were given. It is also apparent that immaturity does not lead to people who match up on the binary congregating, but that people who have complementary functions do.

It's easy for people who have the same pair of rational functions to communicate, as they both perceive the world in similar ways.

An INTJ and an ESFP will usually have an easier time getting on the same page than an INTJ and an ISTP. This is because both the INTJ and the ESFP use the same system to take in information, even if they do the steps in different orders. They simply need to relate to their own past experience to understand the other's position. However, between the INTJ and the ISTP, there's a gap of communication as the ISTP relies on Introverted Thinking while the INTJ communicates through Extroverted Thinking. This also means that the INTJ relies on Introverted Feeling while the ISTP relies on Extroverted Feeling. All of their functions of judgment are incongruent.

This doesn't mean that there can't be great communication between an ISTP and an INTJ, but that there is a level of understanding that much be reached. Introverted Thinking and Extroverted Thinking are very different energies. While the ISTP will always want to experiment with things until he masters muscle memory to the point of competency, the INTJ will want proof of a concept's validity before they file it away in their memory. The ISTP relies on physical experience to prove the functionality of the universe around him while the INTJ prefers to prove his points in the light of the consensus of specialists.

However, it's not so simple that only people with the same functions get along. There have been many pairings between INTJs and INTPs, who shouldn't be able to be friends considering they have no functions in common. This is because we don't need a clone while interacting with another person, but someone that we can get along with.

Every archetype is the exact opposite as the archetype with the same middle two letters and opposite extremes. This means that ESFJs have the exact opposite functions as ISFPs. While the ESFJs primary function is Extroverted Feeling, the ISFP's primary function is Introverted Feeling. The difference between an ESFJ and an ISFJ is only in the placements of their functions, but the difference between an ESFJ and an ESFP is that all of their functions are different, in addition to also being in a different order. While the ESFJ relies on

Extroverted Feeling, the ESFP relies on Extroverted Sensation.

Due to this, the difference between the INTP and the INTJ is not only every function that they possess but the order of those functions. While the INTP grows their understanding of materials endlessly, the INTJ has a vision that is a well of understanding which can't be expressed. This is not a position that puts either archetype at odds, granted that the INTP is emotionally mature and the INTJ has patience.

This relationship is actually incredibly potent because it allows for an incredible amount of information allocation. Provided neither the INTJ nor the INTP gets bogged down by trying to prove themselves or demanding proof from their counterpart, then the relationship can flourish. Both are the most equipped for the pursuit of abstract thought, and through developing a beneficial relationship with each other, they almost completely address their philosophical blind spots.

The binary of being Thinkers isn't the reason that these two types get along but through the strength of their communication skills. If both types are mature enough to communicate in a way that doesn't aggravate the other, then there's an incredible relationship to be had. This is because both of them think in entirely different ways from one another.

Being flexible enough to get along in every situation is the benefit of understanding the functions and balancing your relationship with them.

There is no best archetype, nor is there one that is best at communicating. Interpersonal skills come from maturity and practice, not being born charming. The simplest way to get along with others is to get over yourself. You don't need things to go your way all the time. Learn what others are doing, support them in doing so, and try to take part if you can.

The more you can get along with people who are different than you then the more you will be trained to do so in general. If you can have a great relationship with someone who communicates in a language that might as well be foreign to you, then it will be simple to get along with people who are on the same page as you. Resistance makes the muscles stronger.

So approach this understanding from the point of trying to achieve balance. Don't game people to get them to like you, or set up expectations for someone like they're a pet. Know that everyone is unique and that analyzing their archetype is a way for you to learn how you can best communicate with them, but not because you'll gain a secret power or influence over them.

Once you are able to use the system like this, it will naturally follow that you are able to read the archetypes of the people that you are exposed to. Develop your relationship with people who are interested in the theory and see how they utilize the functions in their lives. Once you observe any of the functions in one person your understanding of that function in general grows. No one exists in a vacuum; everyone is a human in the end. If you can get along with a few people, then you have a good chance of getting along with strangers. If even your closest relationships are strained, then it's time to start analyzing how you communicate.

Focus on learning about how people function, not how the archetypes do. Observe the functions being used by the people around you. Grow your understanding of people, not your loyalty to a theory. Ultimately, the important part to cue in is the ineffable experience that humans go through, not to have a checkbook that you can use to judge others. Make sure to be trying to reach a place of empathy, and you'll be guided in the right direction.

❖ Chapter 2 Understanding Archetypes

As discussed earlier, each archetype is its own system of processing reality through the use of cognitive functions. They

are not a list of binary results, such as whether an individual is a Thinker or a Feeler. Humanity can't be simplified to such a minimalistic degree; everything is much more complex than how someone fits in a binary.

So, instead of reading the types as their relationship to the binary, read them for what functions they use. Every ENXP type will have Extroverted Intuition as a primary function and an introverted rational auxiliary function. Every XNXP will have Extroverted Intuition and an introverted rationalist function as their primary and auxiliary pair, although the order will be different as according to the first variable in the archetype, extroversion, and introversion.

This is because the first variable determines whether the archetype's primary function is introverted or extroverted. The last variable determines whether or not the extroverted function will be a rational or an irrational function. The rationalist functions, as discussed, are thinking and feeling. The irrational functions are intuition and sensation.

While considering this, it is important to note that irrational does not mean wrong or immature. Much, if not most, of life, is irrational. Our sensation and our inclinations point to something much larger than our understanding. We cannot write down why sex is so satisfying, nor can we explain how we know where danger is in the city that we live in. These are parts of the human experience that aren't meant to be explained, but that are perfectly valid. They are called irrational

functions because they function beyond our understanding, not because they don't function correctly.

For extroverts, all judging archetypes have an extroverted rationalist function as their primary function, either Extroverted Thinking, or Extroverted Feeling. These types include the ENTJ, the ESTJ, the

ENFJ, and the ESFJ. The perceiving extroverts all have an extroverted irrational function as their primary function, either Extroverted Sensing, or Extroverted Intuition. These types are the ESFP, the ESTP, the ENFP, and the ENTP. When you're reading the archetypes, start with the last two letters to get a basis of what you're dealing with. If you have an EXXJ, then you know that their primary function is either Extroverted Thinking or Extroverted Feeling and that their auxiliary function is either Introverted Sensation or Introverted Intuition.

For introverts the opposite is true. This is because the final variable in the archetypes does not address the primary function, but the primary extroverted function. So, the INFP, according to the logic used to decode extroverts, should be an intuitive lead. This is, and it isn't true, because the INFP has Extroverted Intuition as their auxiliary function, meaning it is how they communicate with the world around them. However, their primary function is Introverted Feeling, which means that they are a rational type.

The same is true for the INTJ, who looks like they should have a rational function according to the logic used to decode the extroverts. However, the INTJ has Introverted Intuition as a primary function and Extroverted Thinking as an auxiliary function. This means that the INTJ is a perceiving type, even though they communicate through Extroverted Thinking.

This system can be confusing, but it is a way to simplify how to observe the interactions of others. An INTP is not known through their expression of Introverted Thinking. Even though it is their primary function, INTPs often develop it by themselves, for themselves, and keep aloof in life. Instead of focusing on analysis they'll end up relying on absurd humor and working with the people around them. This is because their primary social function is Extroverted Intuition, so when they communicate it is easier for them to play off people using their intuition than it is for them to explain their Introverted Thinking to the point that people can adequately understand.

For INTJs the opposite situation occurs. They are deep, deep people who are not thinking as much as they are channeling some sort of inner wisdom. Introverted Intuition is the hardest function to describe. One of the closest parallels that can be drawn is to ancestral wisdom. Within themselves, there is a vision that cannot exactly be explained. Due to this, the INTJ does not try to communicate through Introverted Intuition but instead relies on Extroverted Thinking. As Introverted Intuition is impossible to follow, Extroverted Thinking is one of the most literal functions. It is the function that dominates academic science and other such prestigious systems. Due to this, the INTJs come off as a hyper-rational type, even though they rely more on their inner irrationality than they do on the rationality they manifest into the world around them.

So, through understanding this, we can understand why the archetypes are labeled for their primary extroverted function instead of their primary functions. Introverted functions are harder to observe in people, and while socializing all archetypes are more likely to rely on their extroverted functions than their introverted functions, despite whether or not they are introverted or extroverted.

Now we understand how to read the first and last letters of the archetypes. The first letter determines whether the first function is an introverted or extroverted function, and the last letter determines which function is extroverted. This information also fills out the half of the structure of the rest of the archetype. For example, if you have an EXXP, you know that they have an extroverted irrational primary function, an introverted rational auxiliary function, an extroverted rational tertiary function, and an introverted irrational function as their inferior function. For an IXXJ you know that they have an introverted irrational primary function, an extroverted rational auxiliary function, an introverted rational tertiary function, and an extroverted irrational inferior function. This framework is a great place to start because once you have, it mapped it's just a matter of applying the middle two variables.

If you take your understanding of the IXXJ types and apply that to the ISTJ, you can easily decode the functions. You know that the primary function is an introverted irrational function, and you know that the secondary will be an extroverted rational function. This is easy to remember if you know that the last variable determines the primary extroverted function, not necessarily the primary function for all types. With this information, you can see that the ISTJ has thinking for their rational function and sensing for their irrational function.

As you remember that they have an introverted irrational function for their primary function, you can decode that their primary function is Introverted Sensation. Seeing that thinking must be one of their first two functions, and with the opposite energy, you can easily see that

the ISTJ's auxiliary function is Extroverted Thinking. Now that you have those two functions the other two are easy to find, as the tertiary function is the inverse of auxiliary, so for the ISTJ that means Introverted Feeling, and the inferior function is the opposite of the primary function, which leaves us seeing that Extroverted Intuition is the inferior function of the ISTJ.

Every archetype should be understood through this and not in any other way. The reason for this is that the archetypes reveal the tools that an individual is working with, not how their future will be. There is no reason for any particular type, nor is there a certain path for any type. There have been brilliant artists from every side of humanity, just as there have been brilliant Thinkers from everywhere too. You are not limited by how you were born, but you can always be lifted up by what you were given if you are grateful for what you have.

The functions are the foundation for everything in relation to this theory. Without understanding them, this will be an exercise in labeling people, not understanding psychology. Once you start paying attention to the functions you will realize that the importance isn't in what type someone is, but in how they manifest their functions. This is because people are incredibly complex and you can't predict their actions, but you can perceive it.

Instead of focusing on how INTJs act, focus on the way that they communicate. Gain experience with the other types and see what groupings make sense for you. Some people group the types based on their middle letters, meaning that INTJs would be part of the NTs or the intuitive Thinkers. These types include INTJs, INTPs, ENTJs, and ENTPs. Observe them and see whether you think that they communicate in similar ways because they all share a preference for

intuition and thought. Once you have your understanding of those types, now try to organize INTJs and ENTJs with ESFPs and ISFPs. Put the INTPs and the ENTPS with ISFJs and ESFJs. Notice the way that they communicate.

The benefit by organizing the archetypes in such a way may seem counter-intuitive, but the opposite archetypes actually rely on all of the same functions. This means that the INTJ and the ESFP are using exactly the same functions to communicate, only in different orders than one another. While that might sound like an issue theoretically, most of the time it is radically beneficial.

This is because the inferior function does not work as a weakness, but as a need. The INTJ is not impaired in their Extroverted Sensation, but not as able to make use of it as they are Introverted Intuition. Due to this, the INTJ does not reject Extroverted Sensation but actually craves it. Most of them try to accommodate this by developing their sense of taste. Often INTJs will be attracted to sports cars or beautiful outfits because they want to fulfill that inner desire within them that Extroverted Sensation breeds as an inferior function.

The ESFP is dealing with the opposite situation. While they are naturally gifted at sports, design, and physically manipulating the world around them, they often struggle to find purpose or to build a vision. Just as the INTJ is buried by their own intuition, the ESFP can find themselves endlessly swimming through the world around them, trying desperately to find meaning in what they do, but only finding more activity.

Due to these attitudes in both the INTJ and the ESFP, the relationship between them has great potential for both types. While

the ESFP can provide the INTJ with the presentation, experience, and aesthetics that the INTJ craves, the INTJ can provide the direction, practicality, and purpose that the ESFP desires. This means that communication is naturally conducive between the two types, even though they couldn't be further on the binary.

This is because the archetypes are not supposed to be solid. Everyone should be striving to achieve balance within their lives. You do not learn your archetype to learn your strengths and weaknesses, but your journey towards harmony. Your inferior function is not one that you should ignore or one that is unfavorable towards you, but one that you must comfort and grow to appreciate.

Understanding that, it's easy to see why opposite archetypes are so good for each other. For an INTJ to be happy, their Extroverted Sensation must be healthy. Just as for ESFP to be happy, their Introverted Intuition must be healthy. It's difficult for every archetype to address their inferior function alone, so by having relationships with people whose lead function is the other's inferior function, the individual stands to increase their health, balance, and ability to deal with people unlike themselves.

This doesn't need to be understood at the moment, but everyone does have all eight functions. This means that there are types that are opposites in several ways, such as the INTP and the ENTJ. The eight functions of the INTP, in order, are Introverted Thinking, Extroverted Intuition, Introverted Sensation, Extroverted Feeling, Extroverted Thinking, Introverted Intuition, Extroverted Sensation, and Introverted Feeling. The eight functions of the ENTJ are, in order, Extroverted Thinking, Introverted Intuition, Extroverted Sensation, Introverted Feeling, Introverted Thinking, Extroverted

Intuition, Introverted Sensation, and Extroverted Feeling. This pairing

literally lines up on no function, yet can often work well together due to their similarities in intent. Communication usually relies on the maturity of both types, but a focus on abstract and logical subjects can create a wonderful conversation between the two.

What could be considered true opposites would be the INTP and the ISFP. The functions of the ISFP are, in order, Introverted Feeling, Extroverted Sensation, Introverted Intuition, Extroverted Thinking, Extroverted Feeling, Introverted Sensation, Extroverted Intuition, and Introverted Thinking. These types have almost nothing in common, and so it is less often that you can perceive relationships easily forming between INTPs and ISFPs than you can perceive between ENTJs and INTPs. This is because although the INTP and the ENTJ do not have a common language, they have common motivations. They both want to build in abstract and reasonable ways. The ISFP has nothing in common with the INTP, even though they are the ISFP is the inverse of the ENTJ. This is because the focus on the function in the ISFP is on a concrete and personal emotionalism. The ENTJ can benefit heavily from this perspective because it is a piece of themselves that they often neglect, but the INTP cannot relate. Not only do they often completely tune out from sensation, often forgetting to shower or clean their room, but they also have a very indirect relationship with their own sense of feeling. They're not the type to care about their own emotions, not because they neglect them, but because their personal feelings aren't what interests them. ENTJs, on the other hand, do tend to neglect their emotions, which do end up being important to them.

There's another theory that would place the INTJ as the true opposite for the INTP as their functional stacks are completely mismatched, meaning that while the INTP has a rational primary function, the INFJ has an irrational primary function. However, theorizing can be endless.

No matter how you cut up the functions and understand them, the point is that what are perceived as opposites are much more similar than they are thought to be. There is little difference between the ways an ESFJ an INTP think, only a difference in emphasis.

This is why one must consider the functions instead of the titles of the archetypes. By organizing the archetypes in accordance with the middle two variables you misunderstand the truth behind the way that the functions are organized. Don't worry about the shadow functions for now, as they are a different subject, but now it is understood that if you take the XSTX types, then you will have two pairs of two types with the same functions, but that those two sets will have opposite functions from one another. Thus, categorization will not be incredibly useful in understanding or predicting behavior. Those types will most likely get along with one another, but they will most likely not act like one another.

So organize the types by function. For example, ISFJs, ESFJs, ENFJs, and INFJs all have Extroverted Feeling as their primary or auxiliary function. This means that all of these types are socially drawn, relying on input from the world around them, while also not being entirely authentic. All of these types are prone to go along with the feelings around them, such as partying, enjoying a certain author or artist, or remembering something fondly if others do, even if their personal experience with it was negative. This grouping also reveals that all of them have Introverted Thinking as either a tertiary or an inferior function. Due to this, you can tell that all of them have a desire for independence and their own interpretation of the world around them, but that they prefer to hide such thoughts underneath an agreeable exterior. Knowing this will help you prepare to interact with these sorts of people, as often people are tricked by Extroverted Feeling.

They see the displays of warmth that every type with it exudes as an authentic embrace of the people around them, thus including the person who is interacting with them. Often the types with Extroverted Feeling are judged as shallower than they really are because it's so easy to get along with them.

If you understand that then you can work past the pleasantries and try to engage with the thoughts that they honestly have.

This comes off as respectful to the Extroverted Feeling dominates because most people treat them like wallpaper. They're easy to get along with and agreeable, so people tend to talk over them. By using their willingness to talk to others about what they're interested in, you communicate that you are interested in them as an individual, not an experience. ESFJs, ISFJs, ENFJs, and INFJs will all appreciate this deeply. They tire of being considered good listeners with nothing to say.

Categories like this also benefit from making Venn Diagrams instead of binaries. The INFJs and the ENFJs are part of the group that uses Extroverted Feeling, but both are also part of the group that uses Introvert Intuition as either their primary or secondary function. This puts them in the same grouping as INTJs and ENTJs. Instead of being perceived by others as similar type, all off these types can rely on their inner need for silence and reflection. They are prone to go through experiences that can be compared to being spoken through by a spiritual power. The INTJs and the ENTJs will express this differently than the INFJs and the ENFJs, but all four of them rely heavily on a personal sense of vision.

By grouping the INFJs and the ENFJs a lot can be seen about their character. Due to them belonging to the types who rely on Extroverted Feeling both types are prone to expressing themselves in accordance with the environment around them. They are slow to create disharmony, although they often have criticism, regardless of whether they voice it or not. Different than the other pair that they share Extroverted Feeling with, INFJs and ENFJs use Introverted Intuition to fill in the gaps of Extroverted Feeling. It is through their reliance on Introverted Intuition that they are able to seek out aesthetics, form their criticisms, and create a world view. The ENFJs will rely more on the atmosphere of the environment that they are in, playing into creating it and maintaining the moods that are already present, hopefully allowing ideas to flourish in the process.

The INFJs will rely more on that inner vision, and try to find the proper people to share that vision with so that it can come into fruition.

By analyzing the different groups that archetypes fit into you can get a much better overview of them instead of making simplistic categories. Just as the individuals are fluid within the types, the types are fluid within themselves. None of this should be insisted on, only observed.

The final thing to mention about the archetypes is that there are different expressions of those archetypes. This means that an ESTJ may fully be an ESTJ, but with a stronger relationship to Introverted Sensation than they have to Extroverted Thinking. Although it may seem like this makes the ESTJ an ISTJ it does not, because they can still fit within the archetype while being developed differently. The biggest difference in the ESTJ with an overdeveloped Introverted Sensation and an ISTJ would be the different function pairings they rely on.

All functions with the same direction are complimentary — for example, Introverted Feeling pairs well with both Introverted Sensation and Introverted Intuition. In healthy individuals, this creates a harmony that promotes strength as the functions learn to accommodate the various weaknesses of each other. When the individual isn't so lucky, then the situation is different. Instead of being complementary functions, the matching functions end up creating a loop.

With the ESTJ their complementary functions would be Extroverted Thinking and Extroverted Intuition. If they balanced their life and matured healthily, this would provide a powerhouse of information for the ESTJ. They're constantly able to sort information while also being able to take in new material to sift through regularly. Their ability to amalgamate and pursue content is unmatched when they're on top of their game. However, it's important that they have a balance with their other functions, namely Introverted Sensation and Introverted Feeling.

If they don't develop these functions than the loop between Extroverted Thinking and Extroverted Intuition will command all of the resources and attention of the ESTJ, leaving them constantly working with no room to address their own lives.

The story of the ISTJ is much different. Their complementary functions are Introverted Sensation and Introverted Feeling. When they're at their best, they are the true preserves of society and family, capable of remembering legends and myths long since forgotten by others. These are the people who make sure that art collections are preserved through economic hardship. Without maturity, there's no grace to this though, and they end up spoiling away locked in their sentimentality. Their loop leaves them unwilling to engage with the world, and too infatuated with their memories.

So an ESTJ with either an overdeveloped or a dominate Introverted Sensation would look similar to the ESTJ. They may need more time to recover than most other ESTJs, and they may have a deeper sense of history, but their issues remain the same. If they don't take care of themselves, then they find themselves extending into overactivity, taking on way more than they can handle. That's one of the sure ways to tell if they are an ESTJ with a strong Introverted Sensing or if they are an ISTJ. If they're prone to the problems associated with the Extroverted Thinking Extroverted Intuition loop, such as hyperactivity and scattered projects while completely forgetting themselves, then they're likely an ESTJ. If they're prone to the problems associated with the Introverted Sensing Introverted Feeling loop, such as withdrawing themselves for extended periods to rot within nostalgia and neglecting their responsibilities, then they're likely an ISTJ.

If they resemble the ESTJ and they still rely on Introverted Sensing either as much or more as Extroverted Thinking, then they can be referred to as ESTJ-Si. These types are rare, so they will not be discussed deeply in this book, but they are a reality and an interesting one. They are highlighted to bring up that the structure of the archetypes is accommodating, and that each is more complicated than a single profile on them. Keep in mind that if someone resembles an archetype except for a few habits, then there's a chance that they rely on their auxiliary function more than others within the same archetype.

It's also of note that some individuals have such powerful function pairings that it's difficult to read which one is their dominant. Using the ESTJ, it's hard to analyze them when they're unhealthy and bursting with energy, as they can dip into their Extroverted Thinking

Extroverted Intuition pair so heavily that they can be read as ENFPs. So instead try to focus on which complementary functional pair individuals use, because if you could sense both Extroverted Thinking and Introverted Sensing within the primary habits of the ESTJ, you would know that they'd be either an ISTJ or an ESTJ.

Even if you couldn't tell if their primary function was Extroverted Thinking or Extroverted Intuition, usually it's easy to tell that they use Introverted Sensing more than Introverted Feeling. While the tertiary function can be overdeveloped in relation to the auxiliary function, it's very rare for the inferior function to be developed more than the auxiliary. Once you knew that they were using Introverted Sensing as their introverted function, you'd know they'd have Extroverted Thinking as their primary function. This is because if the auxiliary function is an introverted perceiving function then the primary function needs to be an extroverted judging function, and vice versa.

You only need to understand what pair of functions a person uses primarily to understand their type essentially. The difference between an ISTJ and an ESTJ is only in order of function. Once you know that they're XSTJ, you know the language that you can expect to use to communicate with them.

❖ Chapter 3 Analyzing Cognitive Functions

There are eight cognitive functions, four rational, and four irrationals. Every individual has all eight, and balanced individuals know how to balance their relationships with the various functions in a harmonious way.

The irrational functions are the ones that address the ineffable experiences in life. Ultimately potential and sentience can't be explained. There are various experiences, such as gut feelings, your consciousness, and aesthetics which have an importance that cannot be put into words. It has to be understood through the other faculties that we have, the ones that do not require language.

These faculties are the faculty of sensation, which is the body communicating itself, and the faculty of intuition, which is either psychic or subconscious. Everyone relies on both of these faculties, and heavily on at least one. We don't exist for papers or time sheets;

we exist to explore, to breed, and to eat good food. Humans live for the experience and because life feels like a gift, not because we understand that it's our responsibility. This experience is an irrational one, but an insanely profound one, and one that is central to the identity of most people. There are few people who have never had a spiritual experience in their life. It is not important if there are spirits or a deity, but that throughout history, and today, people still feel like they are in communion with something higher than themselves. That has gone on before language, and it won't stop until the species does. There will always be believers, and we will always have sensation.

Sensation and intuition both have an introverted and an extroverted form. This is true of all of the functions. While some functions might deal with the same dimension, the introverted and extroverted iterations of those functions often couldn't be more different. This is why it's misleading to group archetypes based on the middle two letters in their shorthand.

Introverted Sensation is the function which drives nostalgia. This isn't commercial nostalgia either; there's no aesthetic to it, there's just an honest attachment to the past and a great memory for it. Emotions and scenes live on in Introverted Sensation, providing both pleasant memories and a wealth of information to rely on during decision making. It is the function through which the individual stores and preserves memories.

It has a unique position as a tertiary function, as it is one of the functions ablest to lead to a loop. This is especially true for both INTPs and INFPs, as if they do not develop their Extroverted Intuition then they will be prone to over-relying on Introverted Sensation. This will leave them chewing over the same information that they have already gathered obsessively with their primary introverted rational functions. It keeps them sentimental, stubborn, and unable to motivate themselves while they need to be exposing themselves to new ideas. However, just as much as it can serve as fuel for self-destruction, it can also be an incredible, if not explosive, source of motivation for the healthy INXP types.

When Introverted Sensation is given too much responsibility, then it leads to nostalgia and cyclical thinking. If it is relieved by other functions, such as Extroverted Intuition, then it can prove instead to be a source of health, inspiration, and meaning. Unhealthy INXP types try to force Introverted Sensation to contain all of the knowledge of the world within itself. This means that they will dig at their own experience for general understanding when that's not what Introverted Sensation can supply. That's the burden that Extroverted Intuition carries.

Without that burden, and with self-worth, then Introverted Sensation serves as the function that defines home, tastes, and comfort. It allows INXPs to build the things that they want to build, and to feel like that they are gaining in their ever-expanding rational understanding of the universe around them. Within Introverted Sensation is the self. It remembers how you take care of yourself if you thought about how you prepared your outfit for yourself, and how you're sleeping. It is the function of health communicating to the body.

ISTJs and ISFJs illustrate this function through their loyalty, their understanding of themselves, and their understanding of their surroundings. They are often people who are slow to talk, but that have a lot to talk about. It is a deep function which has a lot to draw from and is able to provide both comfort and competence.

Extroverted Sensation is the function of presence. While Introverted Sensing is about burning incense so that your body relaxes and you feel like you respect yourself more, Extroverted Sensation is about the smell of that incense. It is about evaluating things for how they are, how they feel to the touch, and how they act.

Due to this, the types with primary or auxiliary Extroverted Sensation tend to be active individuals. The ISTPs are the engineers; the ISFPs are the artists. Even the introverted archetypes that rely on it keep themselves busy by engaging with the world, by doing things that have a beginning, middle, and end.

The ESTPs and the ESFPs are often the most active in a conversation without really having a good grasp on how to present themselves. They're prone to being focused on what's in front of them and struggling to track down things that can't be explained visually or physically. However, to balance this out, they are incredibly physically gifted.

Extroverted Sensation is driving, it is sports, it is dressing well, and it is everything that makes you aware of having a body and receiving attention. It is the function through which the individual expresses their existence, the declaration of their being through proof of doing. As a primary function, it leads to people who are either smooth or unceasing. Both end up being charming, either through their prowess or through their poise.

The archetypes with Extroverted Sensing as a primary function tend to be relaxed, confident individuals that are quick to be alerted. They know how to relax literally, they know how to calm themselves down and how to feel good, but they don't know how to be unaware of their surroundings. Whatever information they're receiving with their senses will be processed, and they will be among the first to respond to stimuli.

As an inferior function, Extroverted Sensation is expressed by the opposite manifestation when the archetypes are immature. Young INTJs and INFJs both struggle to figure out how to carry themselves and what they enjoy doing. They often have art that they enjoy, usually appreciating the texture, but aesthetics can be difficult for them. Their approach to aesthetic is usually involved with a heightened sense of taste, so they are attracted to expensive things even while they're finding their sense of style. This leads them to either overdressing or neglecting their aesthetics as they try to match an idealized aesthetic.

Their sense of spacing is also often off. Although they benefit from partaking in and enjoy physical activity such as dance, golf, and other such things, both the INTJs and the INFJs tend to struggle with knowing where to stand around others, how to manipulate space, and how heavy things are. Extroverted Sensation is the function which modulates physical understanding through the individual's presence.

Introverted Intuition, the lead function of INTJs and INFJs, is the opposite of Extroverted Sensation and is the most difficult function to describe. It works in a way that's deeply personalized and abstract. Often it manifests as a vision, where Introverted Intuition allows a look into the truth beyond reality. Some feel more in tune with the future while doing this, feeling like they are accessing a vision that is slowly being realized as life progresses.

More commonly this function works as various hunches. An INTJ is excellent at understanding information and working with it due to Extroverted Thinking, but it is through Introverted Intuition that the INTJ sorts through that information. Data by itself is meaningless. A dictionary must have words worth forming into sentences for it to have value. For the INTJ this value is perceived through their intuition, and they can see what's important behind the knowledge in front of them. Often, this manifests by the INTJs believing that they can see God through science or history. Introverted Intuition lets them see beyond the data, and perceive importance that's not immediately apparent.

INFJs work similarly but using Extroverted Feeling as their way to assimilate new information. Using their surroundings and the feelings for others, INFJs are able to interpret the key feelings that are manifested around them. Like how the INTJs see God in science,

often the INFJs find gods in the world. They are prone to spiritualizing emotion and seeing that as a deeply motivating force that is the motivation behind reality. This allows them an unexplainable insight into the world around them that runs deep and is a rich source of empathy and consideration. However, when this isn't balancing the INFJs become lost in their own opinions, and they may think over reality. This means that they will insist on their own interpretation of reality instead of listening to the people they are interacting with. When they disagree, they get stubborn and shut down input from the outside world, which sometimes results in them being poor communicators.

INTJs suffer from a similar issue if they don't find balance. Without input from others, INTJs are quick to become arrogant and unwilling to validate the right of others to contribute. They can become too obsessed with facts and box out people through the proofs that they have constructed beforehand. The INTJs are the archetype that is the most prone to autism.

This may help to reveal the nature of Introverted Intuition. It is not a perfect function, but it is a fascinating one. It can be the source of great insight, and the function can channel incredible beauty, but it can also be isolating and unwilling to accommodate others. Just as it is a hard function to explain, it's hard to explain things to the function. Introverted Intuition is almost like an inside joke between an individual and themselves. It is a wonderfully potent language that can describe ineffable things, but it is a language that can't be voiced.

Extroverted Intuition is a much easier function to observe because it is essentially the function of imagination. The function reveals the potential in the world around it, leading individuals with it as a primary function to perceive the world more for what it could be than what it is. ENTPs are incredibly prone to be lost in projects, buried under scraps of things that they started and stopped because they don't see life for how they're living, they see the world as an incredible wealth of resources.

Their brains are always firing away at new ideas, new ways that things could be applied, different ways to have conversations so to be more efficient, and absurd premises that are sure to get laughs. They constantly process what the things around them could be.

ENFPs do something similar but without the practical push behind it. As the ENTPs find themselves in engineering, the ENFPs find themselves teaching art. Their expression of Extroverted Intuition tends to be much more social than the ENTPs. Instead of using

Extroverted Intuition to root through information that Introverted Thinking can turn into experiments, the ENFP uses Extroverted Intuition to reveal information about the people around them.

They perceive the atmosphere behind environments, the motivations that keep certain individuals going, and other such sensitive details. Often they can appear psychic with their uncanny ability to pick up on the emotions of others around them, despite not having Extroverted Feeling.

This is because the ENFPs have such a powerful connection to the world around them with Extroverted Intuition that they appear to be on the exact same page as others.

For all of the other archetypes that have it as a function, Extroverted Intuition remains pretty visible. Even ESTJs give off the impression of that function when they're on a roll, as it pairs so easily with the other extroverted functions.

Extroverted Intuition is one of the most common functions used in communication because it unites archetypes including the INTPs, the ENFPs, the ESTJs, and the ISFJs.

Through having this function at all, most individuals in these archetypes find it incredible to follow Extroverted Intuition and what someone is trying to express with it. It can be understood as a capacity for irrational conversation or understanding what people mean even though they didn't say it literally. It is a sense for how to get along with the world.

The rest of the functions are the rational functions, which have to with the literal aspects of communication. As Extroverted Intuition reveals what people mean abstractly, the rational functions are responsible for the concrete illustrations of their intentions. These functions are the functions of feeling and thought, and both works to define truth.

Extroverted Feeling serves as a powerful function in public.

The need to look like others do, to fit in with societal norms, and to have pleasant small talk are all signs of humanity's engagement with the function. It also works as a way to process emotion in general, as some individuals struggle with what our society has referred to as authenticity. Some people don't know how to react to the emotional stimuli in their life, and these tend to be people who rely on Extroverted Feeling, as it through the reaction of their community to certain occurrence that they can gain an understanding of how to react to those stimuli.

This works as well as authenticity because the important aspect of dealing with emotions is to deal with them maturely, not with an artistic touch. Finding an understanding of feelings through the people around you is just as valid as coming to an understanding through your relationship with the world around you.

Extroverted Feeling gives a sense for understanding feeling through a way that is connected with others, which doesn't make it phony, but empathetic.

ESFJs and ENFJs are archetypes who can often be described as self-forgetting. They find themselves motivated to communicate with others and find it to be important to keep harmony and a willingness to work together. Their fault is in often forgetting to stand up for their own interests or beliefs in the interests of the larger social environment. When they are able to stick by what they think, then they often find it easy to express themselves, as support is easy to find for both ESFJs and ENFJs if they believe in themselves. Their ability to get along with people also serves as an ability to convince others.

For the types that rely on Extroverted Feeling as an auxiliary function the utility of the function immediately changes. While ENFJs and ESFJs are honestly invested in ambiance, harmony, and the emotional health of the settings that they inhabit, INFJs and ISFJs often have different motives. Those types with Extroverted Feeling as an auxiliary function tend to use it as a cover, disguising themselves as agreeable and invested while they really are motivated by their own reasons. Both the INFJs and the ISFJs have Introverted Thinking as a tertiary function, which can be paired with their primary perceiving functions to process information. This means that they are exceptionally capable of receiving and interpreting data, which they can also easily obtain through using Extroverted Feeling. While they are both feeling types, they may be the most misleadingly labeled as both ISFJs and INFJs can be tremendously cold.

The archetypes with Extroverted Feeling as their tertiary or inferior functions are very revealing. Instead of often making use of it, it mostly shows as a deep need in archetypes such as the INTP, the ENTP, the ISTP, and the ESTP. These archetypes tend to be incredibly self-sufficient but in terms of productivity. They're obsessively focused on their interests, but neglectful of their personal needs.

This allows them to be easily manipulated or nurtured by someone who can supply them with Extroverted Feeling. When these archetypes do develop Extroverted Feeling for themselves they often also do it after getting over disdain for public opinion. The result is a journey towards authentically understanding the people around them and embracing the lifestyle of the people who surround them.

Introverted Feeling is the function that is responsible for good and evil. This does not mean societal norms or getting along with others, but a personalized understanding of morality. INFPs are known to be the poetic archetype as they are prone to intense emotion that has no explanation other than passion and previous familiarity. They don't evaluate the world for how others react to it, but their own history. It's an incredibly individualistic perspective because it takes on the weight of morality on the individual.

ISFPs do something similar, although without the same sense of being responsible for abstraction. Instead, they tend to be the artistic archetype, as their feelings about the world around them can become an incredibly profound abstract language through their interpretation. Often they find themselves attached to certain kind of curves, different color palates, and atmospheres. Both ISFPs and INFPs collect resources from the world around them, and then they go through the process of defining what is good and avoiding what they consider evil. It is a powerful sense of judgment because it stems from the self, and poets from Shakespeare to Dante have used this function to paint moralities that the rest of us can perceive and celebrate.

For INTJs and ISTJs this function works as more of a blind spot that must be addressed. As they are incredibly focused, pragmatic types, they often get to a point where they forget to take care of themselves and to develop a relationship with themselves. This means that as they get older, it will be important for them to find art that they enjoy or places in nature that feel like home to them. Introverted Feeling is the function of communicating with yourself in a way that's sensitive and understanding. Even for ESTJs and ENTJs, they will find themselves having to take time to nurture themselves as life progresses. There is no way to address Introverted Feeling without reckoning with the self and having an authentic connection to what could be considered the soul.

Ultimately Introverted Feeling and Extroverted Feeling fulfill similar roles, as they are usually the functions that end up motivating people, either through a desire for harmony or a sense of righteousness, but they are very different functions. This is why it's misleading to categorize all of the feeling archetypes in one group. An INFP and an ENFJ will have a very different sense of what makes emotions valid and what their worth is. Not all feeling comes from the same place; some people honestly are affected by what others think; others only consider themselves when processing their emotions. There is not a simple dichotomy between thinking and feeling, and there is more synergy between thinking and feeling than there is between the different types of feeling. It truly is almost a difference in language.

Extroverted Thinking pairs perfectly with Introverted Feeling, as it takes on the proofs that others have supplied and makes them concrete. In communication Extroverted Thinking is a hyper-rational function, insisting on proofs and history to prove claims. It can work as a dictionary or as a science for the archetypes that make use of it as a function. The reason why it pairs so well with Introverted Feeling is that Introverted Feeling has massive blind spots. It is an incredibly sensitive and beautiful function, but ultimately it can become too self-involved. INFPs and ISFPs tend to run into a problem where they are not truly taking others into consideration, only their own feelings about the people and environments that surround them. Extroverted Thinking works to balance this out as they mature, however, as they will start to understand that their feelings require proof and that their own passions aren't reason enough to act.

ENTJs and ESTJs are powerhouse archetypes. They are the kind of people that drive philosophy in the case of the ENTJ, and society in the case of the ESTJ. Extroverted Thinking could be argued to be the most useful function in terms of creating systems that work in the world. Not only are Extroverted Thinking leads incredibly at taking in new information, but they're also excellent at organizing that information into useful chunks that they can utilize in their lives.

They're prone to throwing out information that doesn't immediately makes sense, which might leave them a bit closed mined, but it also saves them an immeasurable amount of time. Extroverted Thinking is the function of working together, of getting humans motivated to be a part of a team and to share their knowledge to become the best that we can possibly be as a species.

For the types that indirectly make use of this function, like Extroverted Feeling, it usually means something different. INTJs and ISTJs are also interested in public development and utility but are often more motivated by their own interests and ideas. Both of them use Extroverted Thinking to communicate their ideas, but they're also more prone to go with their own hunches than the public consensus. If the public leads to where they want to go then, they'll be happy to reference them, but if not, they'll stay occupied with their own theories.

For the ENFPs, ESFPs, INFPs, and ISFPs, Extroverted Thinking is usually underdeveloped to be used well but is the language that they will force others to communicate with them in.

All of these archetypes are prone to be caught up in their own emotionalism, communicating their own feelings about things while demanding that others communicate with well-explained reasoning. Understanding this can help you communicate with all of those types because you'll understand that your burden is to make sense, not to express yourself honestly. They're looking for how they feel about your thoughts, not to honestly interpret or consider them.

Introverted Thinking is the last function, and as the types of feeling are very different, the different types of thought are too.

While Extroverted Thinking can be compared to science and the philosophy of Aristotle, Introverted Thinking is a much more personalized process. It can be found among engineers, and philosophers such as both Plato and Socrates, who are considered an INFJ and an ENTP respectively. This function specializes in proof that the individual can supply.

When Socrates went around Greece, he went to everyone who claimed to know something and then asked them to explain what they knew. As they did so, he'd ask questions and ask the speakers to define the terms that they were using. This style of conversation got basically everyone to admit that they had no true understanding of what they were speaking on and that they were just posturing to look impressive. Revealing this is why Socrates was executed.

Introverted Thinking is the function of focus and consideration. It tends to be obsessive and focused on true and false, just as Introverted Feeling is focused on good and evil. Often Introverted Thought can dip into the realm of morality, but it's more common that it's motivated by observable reality than it is by passing judgment on others around the individual. Like Introverted Feeling, Introverted Thinking is meticulous, and it wants a perfect understanding of the subject material, not necessarily something that can be explained.

Ironically this results in INTPs, ENTPs, ISTPs, and ESTPs who are better at talking about their feelings due to their tertiary or inferior Extroverted Feeling than they are at sharing their thoughts due to Introverted Thinking being so difficult to translate into understandable language. A similar situation happens with ENFPs, INFPs, ESFPs, and ISFPs where it's easier for them to talk about academic subjects or research due to their tertiary or inferior Extroverted Thinking, and the difficulty that comes from expressing Introverted Feeling directly.

Still, just because a function can't be expressed doesn't mean a function is useless. Einstein relied on Introverted Thinking, and he was still able to be one of the most important figures in modern scientific history. He was also very talented at sharing his thoughts with others, both through his Extroverted Intuition sense of humor, and his Extroverted Feeling sense of connection to humanity. All functions serve a purpose, even if their utility isn't as easily observed as some of the other functions.

For the ISFJs and the INFJs Introverted Thinking can become an incredibly potent function as it pairs with their primary functions. Both Introverted Sensation and Introverted Intuition are deep, rich wells of information that can feed Introverted Thinking for days. If a healthy loop is formed then ISFJs and INFJs can be some of the most logical archetypes within the Feelers, able to both get along well with others and to pursue their own thoughts and interests.

As for the ESFJs and ENFJs, they can benefit from Introverted Thinking just as INTPs and ISTPs can benefit from Extroverted Feeling. Both pairs of archetypes are built to accommodate and nurture their inferior function, especially if they are socially apt.

Those are the eight cognitive functions, as discovered by Carl Yung. The shorthand for the functions is incredibly useful, as it saves space, but it also allows patterns to be seen easier. The shorthand is the first letter of the type of the function capitalized, whether it is Feeling or Sensation, and the first letter of the direction of that function in lowercase, whether it is an introverted or extroverted function. Thus, Extroverted Thinking would be referred to as Te as it is the Thinking Function with an extroverted direction. Introverted Thinking would be written as Te, as it is the Thinking function with an introverted direction. The rest of the functions work in the same system.

So, going in order of Extroverted Thinking, Introverted Thinking, Extroverted Feeling, Introverted Feeling, Extroverted Intuition, Introverted Intuition, Extroverted Sensation, and Introverted Sensation, the shorthand for the functions, in that order, is Te, Ti, Fe, Fi, Ne, Ni, Se, Si. This system will make the archetypes easier to breakdown because it's much easier to memorize these functions than the theory behind typology.

With an ENFJ you know that their primary function is Extroverted Feeling, and you know that their secondary function is Introverted Intuition. With this, you can reveal their dominant function pairing, Fe-Ni.

This gives you a better sense of how the archetype functions than the label ENFJ does, but it also reveals the rest of their functions. As Ni is their auxiliary function that means that Se must be the tertiary function as the tertiary function is the opposite of the auxiliary. Given that you now know the ENFJ is Fe-Ni-Se, it's easy to realize that the last function is Introverted Thinking, both because the inferior function must be the opposite of the primary function and because you have no other options left. This reveals the ENFJ to be Fe-Ni-Se-Ti. You should be able to decode archetypes quickly once you have these principals down.

The reason for this it's much easier to see the patterns within the archetypes once they're spelled out. The ENFJs are Fe-Ni-Se-Ti. The INFJs are Ni-Fe-Ti-Se. ISFJs are Si-Fe-Ti-Ne, and INTPs are Ti- Ne-Si-Fe. ESTJs are Te-Si-Ne-Fi, and INTJs are Ni-Te-Fi-Se. The patterns between these functions are much easier to observe than it is to memorize that extroverted judgers and introverted judgers have opposite functions, but that extroverted judgers and introverted perceivers have the same sorts of order to their functions, although in different directions.

Once you see the functions spelled out for yourself then this information will become second nature to you, and you won't need to memorize anything, you'll gain a feeling for how the types are structured, and what each type has uniquely in common with other types, and the differences they have from the rest.

❖ Chapter 4 Constructing from the Elements

After becoming comfortable with the functions, we may start to build and truly engage with the archetypes. This is because

the archetypes are not built by a series of binaries but through the relationships of the functions within individuals. An ISTJ should not be understood as an introvert with a pragmatic and logical worldview. They should be understood as Si-Te-Fi-Ne, which reveals that they communicate logically and intuitively, but that they have a penchant for nostalgic emotion and need to tend to their needs to ensure that they can be healthy.

This model allows us to truly get into understanding the archetypes because it reveals much more information than is on the surface. We assume that we need to know the type of person someone is, but we don't. We need to understand what pairs of functions they're using, and which they rely on.

The different pairing of functions are the dominant functions, and then the complementary functions. The dominant functions of the ISTJ are Si-Te, and the complementary functions are Si-Fi and Te-Ne. Through the dominant function, we can tell that the ISTJ will rely on past experiences that can either be explained or proven in terms that most people agree with. They rely on their own experiences but aim to turn that experience into something that can benefit the collective.

Through the first complimentary functional pair, we know that the ISTJ is also sensitive to their own experience. Although they'd like to contribute to the usefulness of Te and utilize it to communicate and find their place within the world, Si-Fi reveals a type that is sensitiveto their own history.

They're prone to love their friends, their neighborhoods, and whatever else is theirs, forming a sentimentality that goes against scientific pursuit. The secondary pair of complementary functions, Te-Ne, reveals a great potential to put together new ideas and to feed into development in the professional and information worlds, but also a challenge to realize such potential.

Te-Ne as a complementary secondary pair of functions can also reinforce a negative opinion, or a fear, of the world without properly being balanced, and this imbalance could be further solidified by Si-Fi. Understanding the functions and the relationships serves as an incredible source of insight into the way that the different archetypes both process the world and act within it.

Every archetype has a unique pair of dominant functions. The only types that are truly similar are the archetypes that only differ on whether they are introverted or extroverted. This means that ISFPs are the only type to have Fi-Se as their dominant pair of functions, similar only to the ESFPs who have Se-Fi as their dominant pair. Otherwise, each dominant pair is unique and reveals the most about the different archetypes, as it is the relationship between the primary function and the auxiliary function which ends up defining them.

Several archetypes share sets of complementary functions, however. ISFPs and INTJs both make use of Fi-Ni and Te-Se. ENTJs and ESFPs also share both sets of complementary functions. This reveals heavy similarities between the different archetypes that wouldn't be seen without an understanding of the functions.

Both INTPs and ISFJs are prone to be caught in Si-Ti loops, which is why some INTPs barely act like intuitive types, and why some ISFJs can come across as cold and uncaring. This also results in a similarity of thought between the two types that is pretty unique, as both of them are prone to relying on both of those introverted functions.

Most people would expect the INTP to be paired with the INTJ or the ENTJ in terms of how they think, but it's really the ISFJ that has the most comparable thinking habits. This works for all types, as both ENFPs and ESTJs rely on Te-Ne, which can explain both of their styles of communication. All of the archetypes are similar to their opposite types; it's just a matter of where they put the emphasis on their functions.

Obviously, the complementary functions are the ones that line up in direction, as the synergy between them is something that is built into the functions. Often many types fall into over-relying on these functions because they have not made peace with the ambiversion that is within most personalities. To be healthy people need to find a balance between extending themselves too far into the public and withdrawing into themselves. Both extroverted loops and introverted loops can be powerful, productive systems, but they lack so much if they are not balanced with other aspects of an individual's personality.

The complementary functions are Si-Fi, Si-Ti, Ni-Fi, Ni-Ti, Ne-Fe, Ne-Te, Se-Fe, and Se-Te. All archetypes have two of these pairs, and by utilizing both, they can become incredibly balanced people. Si-Fi is the main functional pairing which is possessed by the ISTJ and the INFP, although both the ESTJ and the ENFP also make use of the pairing. Si-Fi is a pairing which focuses on the emotional nostalgia present in an individual's life, their sense of comfort, and sentimental history. It is powerful for bonding, for providing a sense of meaning in life, and for self-care. It can become too hung up on personal experiences, but it tends to provide a rich experience for those who balance it.

Naturally, all types with Si-Fi also have Ne-Te. The types that have this complementary pairing as their main pair are the ESTJs and the ENFPs, who also have the Si-Fi pair. These archetypes are dominated by creative and rational energy, one that can always expand into new subjects, but that comes with either an understanding or a desire to acquire an understanding. It can become a shallow way to pick apart people for information and resources, but with health, it simply provides a wealth of information that comes across more as interested than it does as interrogative. As it is balanced with Si-Fi, it is a rich cross-section of new, logical information with a deep and emotional sense of history. The combination of Si-Fi and Ne-Te provides for a perfectly balanced individual, just as all pairings of functions do.

Si-Ti is the pair of compliments that are shared by INTPs and ISFJs, although also possessed by ENTPs and ESFJs. As discussed above, it leads them to have a similar mode of thought, one that is dominated by personal experience and analysis. While Si-Fi is nostalgic, Si-Ti is similar, but it focuses on the experience instead of the sentiment. This allows both INTPs and ISFJs to have a great memory of their experiences, and their own interpretations of what those experience mean. It is a way of storing information and then a way of analyzing it either to implement or for individual mental exercises.

The opposite pairing of Ne-Fe also proves powerful in both the ISFJs and INTPs, but more prominent in the ENTPs and ESFJs. This pairing of function allows for uncanny leaps to be made while socializing. Through wild ideas of social harmony, Ne-Fe leads are incredibly charming. They are capable of picking up on the feelings of others, interpreting the mood of a room, and to quickly come upwith their own ideas that are inspired by their surroundings.

It is a powerful pairing that encourages lighthearted socialization about any subject that can be discovered or remembered. If it is balanced with Si-Ti, then it can perfectly mix with it, providing an easy to get along with and charming atmosphere to contrast with the obsessive and esoteric thoughts that Si-Ti tends to lead to. It provides a relatable face for the mental wars that INTPs and ISFJs in particular wage.

Ni-Ti can arguably be as esoteric and as obsessive. It is the pairing which is most present in the INFJ and the ISTP, but also present in the ENFJ and the ESTP.

Usually, it's accommodated by a physical hobby which keeps it grounded, but when it's not Ni-Ti can lead anywhere. It has an incredible and unexplainable insight which is further developed by Ti, even if the definitions of the terms they use as their starting premises are unclear. This means that both the ISTP and the INFJ can have ideas that they develop over time, beautiful ideas, but through a lack of showing their work, they will have a great struggle to express those ideas.

Se-Fe is the other pairing that comes with Ni-Ti, and it is the pairing most expressed in the ENFJ and the ESTP. This is expressed through a gracious physicality, one that is social and that plays fair. These types pour into the world but understand that there are limits to their interactions and that they'd rather make others feel good rather than make them feel worse. It is this pairing which allows the Ni-Ti loop to be balanced and externalized, as it gives the most complicated thoughts an attractive body, but Ni-Ti also keeps Se-Fe from being insufferably shallow.

Se-Te is an incredibly manipulative pairing, as it is the pairing that causes things to occur within the world. The types with this pairing are mainly the ENTJ and the ESFP. However, it is also present in the

INTJ and the ISFP. Se-Te takes in massive amounts of sensory information and applies Te to organize it and to make it useful. These are the types that have a vision that they can actually capitalize on because they will force it into existence. It is a stubborn, powerful, and potent pairing of functions. To offset it, ENTJs and ESFPs have Ni-Fi, which serves to reveal the emotional truth behind the actions and thoughts of Se-Te. The INTJs and the ISFPs are the types who use Ni-Fi the most, and they reveal the sensitive nature of such a pairing.

Both INTJs and ISFPs tend to be quiet individuals, always working on some sort of project, whether it's for education or some personal pursuit. They constantly expand into the world but process it through a deep and detached sense of judgment. As they interact with the world to learn what's fair according to the rules, they withdraw into themselves to determine what they believe is fair. It is only through separating themselves from the world that they can begin to value things for themselves and arrive at their own ethical positions.

All of these pairings are part of a pair with another pairing, and that is because all parts of the personality are made to accommodate each other. Biology doesn't often make mistakes, and we became this way for a reason, so it makes sense to find a beautiful structure within human psychology. Every type is perfectly balanced and contains the tools within themselves to become harmonious, happy, and productive.

The last kinds of pairings are the opposite functions, which always come together, so for example, Ti-Fe or Fi-Te. Every archetype with Te has Fi, and every archetype with Fi has Te. Every archetype that has Ne also relies on Si, and every type with Ni also relies on Se. The opposite function of each function come along together, as they bring each other balance. All of the opposite functions are incredibly compatible.

For example, Ni is incredibly limited by it being difficult to explain. It is an irrational function which is not only introverted but often mystic in nature. To have an INTJ or an INFJ openly express about it is rare, they usually only share their true thoughts with the people who they think are on the same page, or with the people who they love deeply. This is a difficult attribute for many INTJs and INFJs to deal with, but their inferior function actually serves as the answer.

Extroverted Sensation is an incredible function for being understood and for displaying things to others. While Ni might have an incredibly deep relationship with a certain symbol, the history of it and the meaning behind that, Se can wear that symbol well and get people to observe it. Se serves a vehicle to express the insights that Ni supplies. It's through the pairing of the two opposites that INTJs and INFJs can find ways to share their incredibly personal and private experience with the world around them.

Introverted Sensation provides a strong sense of history, where ISFJs and ISTJs have a great memory of what they've done and what they mean to them. They're also aware of their health, the way that they're feeling, and other such essential information that every adult needs to be aware of. For these archetypes that information is direct and always being processed by them, for often there is no way that they can feel out of their body.

Extroverted Intuition offers a perfect complement to this because Si can become incredibly boring. Si serves to provide a rich sense of history and to provide an honest sense of nostalgia, but that can become annoying to listen to for most people who don't also share a strong reliance on the function. This is where Ne shines, as it is the complete opposite. It is always bursting into new territory and trying to reimagine the old. ENTPs and ENFPs are people who are prone to hyperactivity because there's always an opportunity for them. They can't stop seeing it, and they can push into it forever. However, just as Si can become boring, Ne can become senseless, so they are a perfect pairing. Ne gives new information to prevent Si from becoming stagnant, and Si provides profundity to the endless stream of information that Ne uncovers.

Introverted Thinking works to give individuals a unique, but tested, perspective on the world. It only trusts what it can observe. INTPs and ISTPs often prove to be among the hardest individuals to argue with because they require either the theoretical or mechanical understanding before they're willing to accept a premise. It is one of the most powerful functions for analysis, but it often leaves the individuals with it as a primary function in a place that's hard to express. Ti builds understanding, but it doesn't give an explanation. An ISTP can have incredible knowledge about how mechanical things function, but they might have no words that they'd offer to explain such processes. The knowledge is stored in something akin to muscle memory.

This is why Extroverted Feeling is such a godsend for those that utilize Ti. Fe provides an actual expression for other people to cue in on, which softens the insistence of Ti on understanding. Instead of being restrained by authenticity, all users of Ti also have an inherent desire to get along and place harmony over winning arguments due to the presence of Fe. They are very sure in their principals, and they have their own relationship with the data and resources that surround them, but after those subjects, they tend to be people who

are incredibly easy to get along with. This is because Fe places emphasis on good conversation and allows Ti to be put on reserve, learning to object when appropriate.

However, this also addresses the issue with Fe, which can be cowardice. ENFJs and ESFJs due run into issues with expressing themselves, as their desire for harmony can lead them to sacrifice their own health for the good of the collective. Ti can save them from this though, as through utilizing it the ENFJs and ESFJs can reveal their own positions and interpretations of the things around them. This will allow them to realize when preserving harmony is obstructing their ability to express their beliefs.

Extroverted Thinking fulfills a similar role as Extroverted Feeling in that it also wants to create a consensus, but the problems that Te primaries run into are different. While Fe leads tend to be forgotten and taken advantage of, Te leads tend to bulldoze over others and not be fully aware of the consequences of their actions. This is because reality isn't moral, but real. For all of the progress that our cultures have made, for all the cities we built, for all the ideals we secured, rivers of blood were split. There is something that can be valued more than human life, and both ESTJs and ENTJs tend to be the types who understand that. Both are incredibly capable of dedicating themselves to projects much larger than themselves for the sake of a good outcome.

This attitude does come with some flaws as not only can it be forgetting of others; it can be incredibly self-forgetting. Te is built to work, not to build an irrational attachment to things which only slow you down. This is why Introverted Feeling is the natural and perfect function to pair with it. As Te focuses on the outside world and how

to understand the rules that dominate it, Fi focuses on the internal reaction to such events, and the individual's personal opinion.

This means as Te discovers new science and data, Fi can react to such data and the implementation of it. Te may understand how to best run a farm for the cheapest costs and a maximum output of meat, but Fi understands that the individual doesn't want to be exposed to creating such an environment in which the unnecessary suffering of animals would be widespread. Fi provides the counter reasoning to the cold efficiency of Te, acting as a natural outlet for productivity obsessed and impersonal people. It gives them the stimuli to realize the true fallout that would occur from their decisions and thoughts.

Introverted Feeling as a primary function runs into its own problems. For the INFPs and ISFPs, this function can be incredibly demanding, dominating how they interact with the world. Most commonly both archetypes are held back by an understanding of morality which gets in their way while making friends and being exposed to different forms of culture. This is where Extroverted Thinking can give to Fi as Fi gives to it. Te serves to either validate or disprove the feelings of Fi, where it looks for the proof that others agree upon to validate the emotions that they are independently processing. As Fi explores into territory that's incredibly personal, Te can tie the individual back to the world and reality, giving a true sense of presence to the emotions represented by Fi.

By itself, Introverted Feeling is a wonderful function for the individual to understand their placement within the world. The function gives many creative people their worldview, as it is through their emotional reaction that they created their philosophies of life. Explaining those philosophies and interpretations may be difficult, but when it can be captured well, the public ends up with gifts as diverse as The Iliad and The Subterraneans.

Understanding all of these pairings and the different functions will leave you well informed about the different archetypes. Seeing the archetypes for the functions that they utilize will equip you with an understanding of others that expands far beyond binaries. Allowing yourself the freedom to analyze people for how they act instead of what you think they are is a great move. It lets you see life for what it is rather than what you want it to be. Don't get caught up in your preconceptions, but allow reality to be as complex as it truly is.

❖ Chapter 5 The River is never the Same Twice

Despite the accuracy of cognitive functions, nothing is predetermined.

Brain scans have revealed that there is legitimacy to the idea that the brain does section itself off and that different people rely on different strategies for cognition. This confirms that there are likely different types of people and that certain habits aren't as unique as one might think.

This means nothing in terms of your own soul, fate, or worth. As a person, you are a unique iteration of the species and deserve to have your own opportunity to contribute to our understanding. There is no benefit to putting yourself in a box and expecting yourself to act a certain way. That will limit you and make your potential become stunted. We all need to understand that we are free from our own conceptions and that we can be whoever we need to be.

The reason for this is because every person is the first person to live their lives. No one knows what tomorrow will be like with certainty. There could be tremendous fires, a change in the atmosphere, the best economic climate in centuries, or commercial space travel within the near future. We cannot be rigid creatures; we are meant to adapt to exciting circumstances and to contribute our creativity to this reality that we inhabit.

So be free with your idea of yourself and build into the things that you might not expect yourself to. If you are a person dominated by thought, then try to invest in your emotional side. Take time to have a bath, or read something that is emotionally rich to you. Expose yourself to the things that aren't within your habits and don't feel bad for doing so. If you're a Feeler, then try to create distance at different opportunities in your life.

Don't accept that you always have to have a sensitive reaction; try practicing your right to be strong and disinterested.

As you learn to treat yourself with respect, recognize that you are more nuanced than a shorthand analysis of your personality. By doing this, you will have a much richer vocabulary with which to examine yourself and the world. Trying to systemize the incredibly complex reality we inhabit will seldom work well. It's better to take advantage of systems as far as they function, then be flexible once we arrive at the limitations we already expected from them.

This is because it allows you not to force your ideas on the people around you. Once you recognize that you're too complicated to be labeled, you won't be prone to labeling others. Everyone is a complex system; everyone is a Thinker, a Feeler, a Sensor, and an intuitive. There is no one without access to all of the functions, and no one without their own habits.

You can't expect certain things from the same sorts of people. Just because your mother was an ESFP who dominated your ability to create your own space doesn't mean that every ESFP is like that. A bad experience with one person of a certain type doesn't even mean you're incompatible with that sort of person; it means you had a personal issue with them. There are truly no bad or good types, just healthy and unhealthy individuals who manifest their personalities as a reflection of their unique psyche.

Certain types are more compatible with other types, but ultimately personal preference goes far further to determine the types of people individuals are attracted to.

Theory crafting can set up perfect relationships with different functions, but theory isn't the same thing as reality.

Ultimately history will always reign supreme. People like who they know and who they've had experience with. Trust is huge in the estimation of others. This will do more to determine who people form relationships with than any sort of typology will. Don't change anything in accordance with typology if it's a meaningful part of your life.

People can become well balanced over time. Even if people are born with certain aptitudes or habits, they can grow out of them. This is true with tics, imaginary friends, social skills, and mechanical skills. Some children only want to tinker with their projects; other children never want to come home. Everyone has their own journey on this planet.

Due to this, an older brother with Extroverted Thinking as his primary function could train his ISTP little sister to become fluent in utilizing Extroverted Thinking. This development of a function that's atypical for the archetype does not upset the natural balance of the little sister, nor does it change her type. Everyone can develop any part of themselves at any time, and it is good to do so.

Most people end up with uneven development in their functions. This is because the functions are listed in the way that they are related to one another, not because they are listed in the order that you use them. Many people are secondary dominant, so they could be an ENFJ with Introverted Intuition dominant function, even though Extroverted Feeling is their primary function.

The reason for this is incredibly complex and isn't explained away through theory in an adequate way. Ultimately, there are billions of people, and they all come to their own ways of living. That is too complicated a process to simplify into neatly divided archetypes that everybody can fit in.

So due to that, we have ENFJs that perfectly fit within the archetype, but they rely more on their intuition than they do their feeling. These are still ENFJs, and that's because ENFJs can be as different from each other as any one person is from another. Diabetic patients do not need to resemble each other, nor do people who have nut allergies. Similarities don't mean that things are congruous.

Active participation will always far outweigh theoretical understanding. You don't need to read types and plan out the ideal conversations;

you need to be able to do basic and quick readings that let you see the style that the people you want to communicate to are communicating in, and then to be able also to practice that style. By doing so you can open up opportunities that most people aren't savvy enough to experience, but if you try to game people, then you'll risk coming off as someone too detached to have a relationship.

Insistence makes you inconsiderate. People will express themselves how they have learned to, not how they should theoretically. Never expect someone to live up to the idea that you have of them, but try to form an idea of who they are.

There are several facets to a human personality. Learning how someone talks about their car may let you observe how they express themselves in general. As you bond with someone, you understand that they have more dimensions and richer dimensions than you could have imagined. Everyone has their own structure, their own taste, and their own conclusions. Typing people can help you

 observe a facet of that person, but as much as any other facet would.

You don't know a person just because of their diet, or how they drive. People have more than one thing to take into consideration. Play with your sense of empathy and understand the unique attributes of everyone that you interact with. Respect people enough to pay attention and validate their right to be addressed.

Apply this standard to yourself as well. Don't become rigid in your thinking because you think you understand yourself. Always welcome growth and be ready to develop your relationship with yourself. If you get too comfortable relying on your strengths, then you won't learn to appreciate them. There are different tools for different situations, and experience will teach you what is appropriate.

When you force yourself to rely on your strengths, you end up having to climb walls when there are stairs right next to them. There are ways to approach life that take less effort than others, and nothing works all the time. Balance leads to the ability to lead a productive and healthy life. Don't limit the conception of your strengths. You can build upon what you have until you die.

Being skeptical of typology is the best way of implementing it. Understand that these categories, like all categories, are flawed, and we are simply trying to make sense of the larger human collective. This knowledge is not to gain true insight into the soul of everyone that you meet, but to gain a playbook for how to handle yourself in social encounters.

Getting along with others is an art form. Everyone likes different things. What is beautiful to one person is an utter bore to another.

Children use these preferences to form cliques and close friends. Adults realize that there are thousands of people with different tastes and experiences, so they don't need to be limited to people who communicate in the ways that they're inherently comfortable communicating. As we grow older, we should become more flexible with the ways that we express ourselves. We age to mature, not to remain however we were born.

As you master recognizing the different types, and the functions that they rely on, the change that occurs should be within yourself. You shouldn't think that now you have an understanding of how other people will act, you should accommodate others with how you act. Your understanding should be in what others are motivated by and are comfortable with. Don't try to game other people, nor try to understand them fully. This is not an attempt to define them.

Manipulation is a bad game, and labeling might be worse. When you engage in these things, you sink to a lower level of acting. You're no longer trying to understand where people are coming from, but where you can get them to go. This energy always backfires, as the best that you can cause is irreparable damage to someone who is close to you. You can't mess with the intentions of other people without harming their ability to trust themselves.

So instead of trying to force others according to your needs, adapt your actions to the needs of others. Don't be a pushover or a servant, but be the first volunteer when you notice that something needs to get done. Volunteering to be flexible is often a sign of wisdom. Most people are too lazy or petty to contribute to a positive outcome. If you are the person to do so, then you are the person who decided to step up.

Use this knowledge to do so, recognize everyone has limits and needs support. There are things that every kind of person can benefit from, and knowing typology well will help you figure out how to supply that support. Understanding the flaws in the system, and that there are people who don't easily fit within it, will allow you to be a person with a wide-reaching and deep understanding of how to communicate with others. You'll know how people speak generally, and how to differentiate the individual from the archetype.

The unique qualities of each person are what define them. They get to be as instrumental as anybody else; life is everybody's journey. Everyone gets their own voice and experience. Respect that and interpret everyone as a new person, never put people in a box that you have previously defined.

Be open to the diversity inherent in our world. There are many different species of plants, there are beautiful and varied landscapes, and there are several planets. The idea that humans wouldn't be as complicated as everything else, in reality, is laughable. There is no true comprehension in our species; the knowledge of all existence will never belong to a single mind. Don't be so arrogant that you think understanding can be owned, it is only reached, if not borrowed.

People will prove your expectations wrong. Reward them for doing so by reacting to it like it's how they should have acted. Don't be rigid in your thinking or else you'll get irritated by what you didn't assemble. It's much more fun to talk to somebody who knows how to be wrong than it is to talk to someone who thinks they know everything. Adults should understand that awe is a crucial part of the human experience. If we do not admit how miraculous our reality is,

then we might forget to appreciate how much attention we should pay to it.

Half the battle is showing up, and complacency leads to accidents. Have confidence, but don't trust yourself to a fault. Observe the situation for what it is, give it your best attention, and be willing to be wrong.

❖ Chapter 6 Psychic Prejudice

The way that the functions are internalized, and the way that the archetypes are expressed, entirely come down to the individual. Some people find it easy to think of intuition as the processof abstract thought, meaning that it is subconscious processing of stimuli based on either the previous experience of the individual or the previous experiences of themselves and their ancestors. Other people are convinced that intuition is interfacing with the divine, that the information one obtains from intuition is the same thing as divination.

No one is right orwrong in their interpretations of the functions, but there are a variety of schools of thought on how everything functions. It's better to understand how the functions work instead of why.

That information you can share, and you can understand. The other sort will only lead to debate.

There are other such heated topics, such as the superiority of certain functions. Many Intuitives struggle to value sensation, just as Sensors struggle to value intuition. This is because they live life in different ways, and are guided by different principals. The Sensors are physical people, more connected to the animal elements of life than the Intuitives.

This leads them to understand the world around them as reality, and because of this, they insist on physical proofs along with demonstration. This can lead them to devaluing the abstract pursuits, and not understanding the merits in imagination.

Likewise, the Intuitives can look down at Sensors for similar reasons. As Sensors disrespect Intuitives for their dreaminess, Intuitives can look down at Sensors because of their lack of cognitive activity.

Sensors live life for life itself, to take part in the grand drama, but that has little to no interests for Intuitives.

Instead, Intuitives live life to be inspired and to gain a greater understanding of meaning and purpose. They see the Sensor lifestyle as a waste of decades, getting better and better at activities while never growing.

Both of these perspectives are wrong. Everyone is valuable and deserving of love. There is no ideal type, just as there are no horrible types. All judgment of the functions is a mere preference, and each is as valid as the others are.

If you struggle with these judgments, then let go of your ego and realize that you are not perfect. No one is a better human than anyone else is. We all were born, we all suffer, and we all achieve. Do not invalidate anybody.

Still, prejudices do a lot to predict how people act and are even more powerful than archetypes. A Christian INTP and a Christian INTJ will usually have more in common than a Christian INTJ and an atheist INTJ. This is because their presuppositions determine how they utilize their functions.

Ti and Te aren't that different if they are both growing to understand God better. Whether or not the information is processed socially or individually is unimportant if the end goal is to bring glory to the same creator.

So, archetypes won't reveal as much to you as other basic attributes of people, such as whether or not they support the family unit. People's opinions are much stronger than their habits, and the Asian

American demographic votes Democrat for the most part, although their lifestyles directly align with Republican values. What people say, and how they identify, is not as powerful as their inherent beliefs. Those will be what truly determine their actions.

Pay attention to those attributes as you try to understand someone. An INFP who believes that the rule of law is the most essential aspect to a functional society will look much less emotional than an INFP who believes that authentic expression is the only way to engage their soul.

These opinions radically change how the individuals express themselves and need to be taken into account.

There are prejudices that are more common among certain type than others, however. For example, the INFPs are prone to getting into arguments which were not intended to be arguments. The INFJs are prone to a similar issue, but for different reasons. In the case of the INFP, their reliance on Fi-Si can lead them to be blinded by their own interpretation of events. Instead of using Ne-Te to accurately interpret the intentions of the other person, which is the strength of those functions, INFPs sometimes forget to listen to others and obsess over their own opinions. This leads them to feel hurt, shutting down, and not engaging with others to figure out how they actually feel about them. They obsess over a few interactions and use that to build their opinions. These opinions can often be oppressive, and keep the INFPs locked away, mourning their emotions.

For the INFJ the situation is similar, but due to a completely different functional pairing. It is through Ni-Ti that the INFJ receives their own interpretation of the world around them. After picking up a vibe through Fe-Se, they are prone to interpreting it with Ni-Ti in a way that was not intended by whoever was communicating with them. The issue with the INFJ isn't that they isolate, but that they completely box out the person who they perceived to offend them.

Once they have interpreted what the other person has said they are very slow to change that interpretation, which means that they will insist that the meaning they heard was the meaning the other person had intended.

The only way to move past this is if the INFJ finally engages with Fe-Se and is willing to listen to the true intentions of the people around them instead of assuming that they already understand the positions of the people around them.

If this does not occur, then the INFJ will continue assuming that they know how others are thinking and will act in accordance with their interpretation instead of reality.

Such blind spots are common for archetypes to suffer from. The INTP and the ENTP are often absolutely awful about taking care of themselves. These archetypes tend to be prone to distraction, always focused on a project or the future as their room smells, their hair is uncombed, and their responsibilities float by.

Most INTPs and ENTPs have no illusions about this, and can fully admit that they struggle to take care of themselves, but many think that self-care is unimportant and that productivity is the only thing that matters.

This mindset is childish, and useless, as it leads to the XNTPs engaging in hyperactivity with too much energy to focus.

Instead of becoming more productive by ignoring their needs, they often limit their ability to be productive by doing so.

What all of the archetypes need to learn is to balance themselves and to rely on all of their tools instead of a few. XNTPs have Si, which would allow them to take proper care of themselves if it was properly nurtured. The prejudice that XNTPs run into is an underappreciation of their own functions, which is a common issue across all of the archetypes. It is often through the strength of a function, such as Ne, that its opposite is forgotten, such as Si. This leads to immaturity and prejudice because, as discussed, every function is paired with its opposite.

The INFP would benefit heavily from engaging with Te as it is through Fi that they end up drowning in strong sentiment. Te is the perfect pull to deescalate their emotional state as it takes a direct and pragmatic approach to reality. While Fi can be convinced that everyone hates them and that they are absolutely hated within their community, Te remembers how they are treated and the conversations they have with others. Most often Te will reveal that the INFP is actually okay, beloved, and totally safe. Our insecurities are created through the unanswered blind spots in our strengths. By addressing our weaknesses, we rid ourselves of ignorance.

Balance is the most powerful thing in life. It gives maturity, strength, understanding, and perspective. Prejudices and intellectual weaknesses often stem from imbalance and nothing else.

An imbalance is enough to make people unwilling to listen, immature, and unable to develop their abilities. This is why it's important to address the way that individuals think before you judge them, as their prejudices often reveal more than their type.

Separate from matters of belief and other such abstract motivations, social prejudice is often revealing of archetypes.

ISFJs tend to hate people who have strong opinions and dreamers who do not have the ability to translate their visions. This is because Si-Ti is a functional pair that focuses on history and analysis, and Si-Fe is a functional pairing that places harmony and someone's standing within a family or community above their competency. Thus, immature ISFJs will have a massive disdain for people who are competent but disagreeable, such as the ISTJs and INTJs.

ISFJs value people who can think and who can get things done, but not if they're sour people. INTPs and ISTPs tend to have a sense of humor that is charming enough for the ISFJs to get along with them, but the sense of humor from INTJs and ISTJs isn't absurd enough or understandable enough for ISFJs to appreciate them.

Te-Fi humor has much more to do with acceptable jokes, such as quoting a TV show, where Fe-Ti humor revolves more around breaking social norms and saying things that are inappropriate, but true to an internally consistent logic.

This is a complicated thing to understand, but once you gain a hold of it, your understanding of all of the archetypes will improve.

The best way to gain information is to practice. Engage with the different archetypes and learn about their habits. Mature and immature individuals within the same archetype will show you a plethora of different expressions of the same functions, which gives you a great source of information to work with while trying to understand the larger type.

Once you can observe them in sickness and health, you will know how they look no matter the season.

Experience will allow you to observe the types in action instead of in theory. It's really not that weird to ask the people in your life to find out what type they are, either they already know and don't mind sharing, or they'll get a kick out of taking some internet test. If they do end up taking a test for the first time with you, then analyze whether or not the typing is accurate, as there is also a lot to learn from the blind spots in the tests currently available.

The largest misconception that people carry is that they are either introverted or extroverted. This is problematic because again, everyone has every function. When people obsess over introversion and extroversion, they are simplifying life to an absurd degree, and are trying to fit into an imaginary box that they came across. Still, this mania for insisting on whether an individual is introverted or extroverted exists, and the prejudice that stems from the fallout is awful.

This leads to leagues of introverts creating online communities on which they complain about extroverts and how we live in the extroverts' world. If it was not for the basics of the theory, this complaint could carry weight. Te, Se, Ne, and Fe do dominate our society and act as the mediums through which we can express to

one another. This is not because of the rule of extroverts, however. It is because these functions are the social functions through which people communicate, and every introvert has one of them as their auxiliary function. These functions dominate because introverts use them too.

The inverse argument could also be made, where it's stated that fiction, art, self-reflection, personal conversations, and dreams all belong to introverts. This somewhat makes sense as it is Si, Fi, Ni, and Ti that are the roots behind most of these activities, but again, every extrovert has one of those functions as their auxiliary function.

Everyone is an ambivert who makes use of more than one function, and that must be understood. The world is not split up between introverts and extroverts, but into a group of people that prefer external stimuli, and a group of people that prefer internal stimuli. Both groups must make use of the other sort of stimuli to stay alive, but they do have their preference. This is all that is meant by the terms introversion and extroversion; there are no teams.

So, instead of falling within that trap, focus instead on who people are, and who you are. This will reveal something much deeper than preferences, as the functions are a system within ourselves that process our cognition. The functions are varied, complementary, and provide a complete worldview when balanced with one another.

The healthier an individual is, the less they will look like either an extrovert or an introvert. Past looks, the less they will act like either, as it is through balance that people are able to spend time meaningfully within the company of others and by themselves.

All archetypes are prone to their own failures, and individuals are even more so. Personal history cannot be discounted when considering the reasons for the prejudices and habits that an individual caries with them. Examine the people in front of you for who they are, not how they present themselves. People often hide their true natures or exaggerate attributes which aren't as pronounced as they make them out to be.

Ultimately, the way that people think is determined by their experience. Some grow up religious; others grow up in a home that is trusting of strangers. Everyone has their own experience, and everyone has their own parents.

Treat everyone like a unique iteration of our species, because they are. We are all the first, and only, us that will ever exist.

Don't emphasis categorization over that or you will lose any hope to acquire a true understanding of others.

❖ Chapter 7 Cold Readings

When you have no history or knowledge to go off, then you have to rely on your ability to read others to pick up information. This is a more difficult position to be in as you have to do all of your analysis within the moment, but it is still very doable, and the more experience you have with reading others, the easier it will become.

Extroverted Intuition serves as an excellent function in cold readings, as both ENTPs and ENFPs tend to have a good social sense. ENFPs often resemble psychics with how much information they are able to pick up from others, and ENTPs are insane with how much information they can glean and get out of people within minutes. If you have a strong sense of Extroverted Intuition, then it will do an excellent job as a guide for how to read others and to perceive their archetype along with their personality.

This works so well because Ne is incredibly similar to empathy. While Fe is harmony or taking on the emotions of an environment to promote peace, Ne understands things from where they come from. Ne is capable of noticing the potential for growth within things because it can imagine where that thing is going to go, and how it got there. This function is similar to taking on the thoughts and feelings around you yourself, as it requires an understanding of the object to predict its path. ENTPs and ENFPs both are great at taking on the attributes of the people they are interacting with, which is why it's so easy for both of them to gain and make use of trust. However, both ENTPs and ENFPs can be prone to over-relying on Ne and thinking they understand more than they actually do.

Regardless, it is a powerful function for understanding others and can serve as a great guide when you have no available information.

Without Ne, Se also suffices as a way to notice information, as will be discussed later. With Ne, the key things to notice will be the habits of individuals, the way that they speak, and their intellectual consistencies. These will reveal a great deal about the person you are trying to learn about, as it is action and lifestyle that we reveal who we are, not through posturing or language.

Otherwise, all of the functions can be useful while trying to pick up information on a stranger. Everybody has their own strengths, so rely on what has served you before to enrich your relationships with people you haven't had as much experience with.

If your Ni has led you into all of your substantial relationships, then trust it to lead you through the future. You are your own person. What works for you will not work for other people. Aircraft carriers can't use sails to navigate, and sailboats shouldn't be used to ship metal.

So trust in your history and your experience. The positive relationships that you have formed in your life are a map to form more. Use them to guide you into the future, and you will repeat the same good fortune that you have found yourself in before.

If you don't have a positive experience with meeting people, then emulate the conversations that you enjoy. Supply the energy that you appreciate while meeting and working with other people.

This will attract the energy that you yourself desire, and the relationships that you initiate will answer the hunger that you carry within yourself for connection.

If you don't want to attract a certain kind of person, but truly deal with strangers, then listen. Don't try to do it right, or learn any strategies, instead simply address the people who are in front of you.

Through conversation, you will be able to pick-up on the needs of the people you interact with.

People willingly reveal themselves to patient people. Whatever someone is thinking or whatever they want to do, they will usually say. This is because most people are honest, and they talk about the things that are going on or the things that they want to happen. Socializing isn't that complicated if you know how to listen to other people and hear them.

Most people struggle with conversations because they make things too complicated. Either they want to give a perfect answer, or they get too hung up on the words that were said. Anxiety ravages their abilities to communicate, and so they either talk too much and bulldoze the original topic, or they withdraw and look disinterested. Either way, it's not an ideal outcome for the interaction.

If you struggle with interpersonal interaction, then take things slower, and simpler. Directly interpret what people say keeping their tone and the situation in mind.

Don't assume hidden meanings or complexities where there are none, instead, let people bring those up if they are relevant. For the most part, people just want people to listen to them. Provide people with an active audience, and they will be satisfied.

To do this, you need to engage with whatever is within yourself that allows you to listen. Most functions can be used to do so, whether it's picking apart things through Ti or contrasting a story to your own experience with Si. Of course, all off the extroverted functions can be used to communicate, but use them passively instead of actively. Encourage the other person to take the lead.

By doing so, they will display their archetype more fully. As leaders, people tend to rely on their strengths, meaning their true strengths instead of the ones that they want to project. As they take responsibility for the conversation, they will need to rely on the things that define them to carry the weight. If you can sense what functions they are using to maintain the conversation, then you can identify their archetype.

Each archetype has its own style of leading, and individuals use the tools at their disposal in different ways. Some ISTPs rely on communicating abstractly about very nuanced ideas; others immediately make use of physical demonstration when they are put in a position where they must explain something. Still, both reactions are typical of the ISTP and will reveal their type if you are able to interpret their actions.

Alternatively, you can take the lead yourself and read them by applying different pressures. This is a more difficult process to pull off than reading passively, as you have to have the finesse and the understanding to target different functions within the individuals directly.

If you're an ISTJ, then you can feel people out through your Si-Fi or your Ne-Te functional pairings. First, you could approach them trying to relate to them by asking them about where they grew up, what hobbies they enjoy, and who their favorite artists are. If that didn't go well, you could shift into Ne-Te and start discussing the laws behind various things, such as a bad referee call that happened in the last local sports game. Both approaches will reveal a lot about the person you're engaging with because their reactions will show their own relationship to the functions.

When you come across someone that completely rejects your nostalgia and talks about their home for how it looks instead of what it means to them, then you're most likely dealing with someone with Se. This is because their nostalgia is rarely associated with sentiment; it has more to do with remembering how things felt, or what they were doing somewhere than it does returning into the emotions of the memory. Realizing this, and observing it in the people around you, will greatly increase your awareness of the function, and how others utilize it.

The person who did this could even be an INTJ because the presence of Se at all in their functional stack means that they are more prone to tangibility than nostalgia. They'd rather see your nice car than talk about how your mother cooked when you were a child.

All Se users have this attribute to them, which is why recognizing it can be so useful while reading others.

Each of the functions has a distinct profile, and so reading them shouldn't be that hard. Once you observe them your ability to recognize them will naturally solidify. There are plenty of descriptions of each of the functions available online that go in extreme detail, but getting a sense for each of the functions yourself will be a more useful exercise. This is similar to learning a language, as it doesn't matter how hard you study a language.

The majority of learning how to be fluent comes from input, which means hearing the language being spoken around you and relying on it for day-to-day functionality. With the archetypes, take a similar approach, and try to learn from observing them around you, not reading about them.

Still, some tricks are helpful in identifying certain functions and archetypes. Fe-Ti arguments tend to be incredibly different from Te- Fi arguments. The way that the archetypes that make use of Fi-Te, including the INTJs, the INFPs, the ENFPs, the ISFPs, and others argue are both personal and objective. Through channeling Extroverted Thinking, these archetypes prefer to argue with a list of references on their side.

They prefer not to enter an engagement unprepared because they rely more on the consensus that professionals have reached than they do on postulation and other mental exercises.

To prove their positions, they may rely on medicine, politics, or other such systems which over rigidity rules. This is because they want to start on ground that is agreed upon instead of arriving there through the conversation.

Arguing like this allows for an emphasis to form around Introverted Feeling in terms of determining what matters in the conversation.

Extroverted Thinking provides the information, a sense of reality, and an agreed-upon history, while Introverted Feeling serves to give meaning to that history and to offer a personal interpretation of the events that had occurred. This is because of the way their functions work. They don't think that different ways of thought are different forms of expression, but instead that there are things that are correct and incorrect. It is a strong societal sentiment that the sum of human knowledge is sufficient to supply explanations and answers in response to the questions of life.

The development of that sentiment is then that the individual gets to have their own emotional reaction to how society functions. It is not their place to challenge the status quo of information casually, but if they feel in their heart that something is out of place, then it is time for them to act.

This way of thinking leads to arguments that are personal and well proven.

They want to lay out the world in a way that is agreed upon and then judge the morality of that world. It is a highly functional form of conversation, as science is hard to argue with, and everyone is entitled to their feelings. Individuals with this pairing tend to be very efficient at what they do, as ESTJs and ENTJs run the world. Even INFPs have an air of efficiency around them, which is often paired with a minimalist presentation of themselves.

The biggest flaw in this argumentative style is how quickly things can veer into the realm of personal disagreements.

If people aren't on the same page, then Fi-Te forces a disagreement, and then Fi can become sensitive and cause them to withdraw from the argument. To speak well within this style, the conversation needs to be kept either personal or impersonal. Otherwise too much is at risk.

Introverted Thinking paired with Extroverted Feeling tends to fuel very different arguments.

Where Extroverted Thinking insists on legitimacy, Introverted Thinking demands explanation. Ti doesn't care where you read something, or who said it, if you can't argue on behalf of it, or explain it; it doesn't matter.

This means that the only way to communicate with them is to represent your own ideas and your own experience.

Immediately this causes problems with those that communicate with Te-Fi because Te wants to work off a scientific consensus while Ti-Fe wants to work off something that can be described as philosophy. These are diametrically opposed views, and communicating between the two different pairings can be strained. Either the archetypes that rely on Te-Fi need to have patience and to appreciate things that aren't written by experts, or the archetypes that rely on Ti-Fe need to find sources to back up their claims and to speak with more authority. Beautiful relationships can form between individuals with either pairing, but often the relationships suffer from communication issues.

When people with Extroverted Feeling argue they either do so hesitantly or to repair the atmosphere of an environment. Naturally, they tend to be conflict avoidant because it's uncomfortable for them to stand up to others. Instead of arguing, they usually opt to try to redirect the conversation to a lighter subject. If they feel that they must argue it's usually because they've bottled up their feelings, or they feel that a principal was violated.

Once triggered, Extroverted Feeling can be awful. It is as capable as projecting negative emotion as it is at projecting positive emotion. Instead of tending to be withdrawn, as people who have been hurt that rely on Fi, spurned types that rely on Fe can get explosive.

They project emotion to absurd levels, being able to raise their voice as an art form, and they act like they're in a court setting once they start criticizing the people they dislike.

They start with how the person is bad for other people, and they don't stop until they've listed every reason, or at least most of the reasons, that they think so.

So, Fe-Ti prefers to express itself through its own reasoning. It doesn't want to work from consensus or the positions of experts, but from what the individual has figured out during the course of their own life. If that isn't respected and they aren't given space, then Fe will kick in, and they will start playing the environment against the person that they are arguing with.

This includes changing their tone and body language, projecting negative emotion, and using the judgments of the community against the individual.

The difference is that while the archetypes that rely on Te-Fi like to consult experts, the archetypes that rely on Ti-Fe like to consult the people that they know.

Te-Fi speaks to science; Ti-Fe speaks to the community. Those that rely on Te-Fi can be considered the global individuals, people who work with universal concepts that they have their own

interpretations of. Those that rely on Fe-Ti can be considered people with universal perspectives, as they work from their own experience and thoughts, but arrive at places that can be understood by most people even if the method used to get there was unorthodox.

Both of these styles of arguing, Te-Fi, and Fe-Ti are easy to notice in others once you start paying attention to it. These functions dominate how people interact with each other, and how they interpret the world around them. Of course, they would be responsible for how people understand others, and how they make themselves understood.

❖ Chapter 8 Body Language

he majority of human expression comes from a combination of gesture and tone. People don't talk like they're reading a book. Words often lose their literal meaning within conversations. Due to this, you are familiarizing yourself more with how conversations feel

than what they mean is a great strategy.

The atmosphere is important to everyone. Si users need a good atmosphere to feel at peace with themselves and comfortable, Se users need a good atmosphere to be engaged and to maintain interest being anywhere. There is no specific archetype that benefits or relies on atmosphere, although there are several that tend to be gifted at culminating it. Still, no matter who you are, you can interpret and benefit from the appropriate use of atmosphere.

Start by thinking about how you speak. The way that you carry yourself will determine the energy that you attract into your life. If you speak with stress in your voice, throwing words out in a quick and shrill voice, then you will chase away the interests that others have in interacting with you. This is because they will mirror your stress and react in the same defensive way that you have. Carry yourself with a strong, stable voice, use simple sentences, and exude patience. Those conversations will shift dramatically.

By learning to make yourself into an agreeable and presentable person, you will help teach others to do so as well. We are our influences, and positive health is associated with having healthy relationships within your life. People learn from others around them, and so they are fussy about who they spend time around. If you appear as someone who is competent and comfortable with how

they spend their time, then others will want that energy within their own lives so they will pursue your attention.

To do this, you may need to heal yourself.

Most Americans suffer from postural problems, in addition to having a poor diet. It's a hassle, but learning how to carry your shoulder and spine properly will communicate great things about you. If you carry yourself as you respect yourself, then people will tend to respect you as well. Life treats you the way you treat it. Addressing your diet will improve your skin, sleep schedule, and irritability.

These physical actions will better your health. Starting here will allow you to implement concrete plans to address your ability to communicate with your body, as your health will change the way that you carry yourself and how you feel about yourself. As this progression occurs, it's natural for you to pick up more confident gestures and to become more patient.

This is because being unhealthy is stressful. If you don't get adequate sleep, or if you have a poor diet, or if you have unhealthy relationships in your life, then it is likely that you're too stressed out.

This will affect your patience, your ability to communicate with others, and your ability to focus. All of these problems can get in the way of body language because your body feels negative. Under stress, the body communicates to the body that things are unideal and that drastic change would be a welcome situation. This leads to an individual becoming paranoid, impatient, and unpleasant.

Therefore, through exorcizing the negative energy in your life, you stand to improve your communication skills. If you suffer from stomach issues or general pain, then that will affect your normal conversation. All negative stimuli, especially if consistent, contributes to your general mood.

If you can repair your health, or find a point where you're comfortable coping with whatever you must cope with, then your standard mood will be much more approachable. You will hold yourself looser and not look stressed.

This is who people want to interact with when they're being social. Everyone prefers an environment that they feel listened to and safe in rather than one that feels stressful.

Not everything needs to be a conversation. Sometimes it's better not to bring things up. That doesn't mean that you need to lie, but that it's not always an appropriate time for every conversation. Depressing subjects and mourning the world should be kept somewhat private. These topics promote unhealthy trains of thoughts and depressive postures, which will further communicate that negativity. Talking about awful things makes you feel awful, as they should. The body understands that words do not communicate meaning, the tone does, and so when you discuss depressing subjects your body emulates the tone and mood that is respectful to such a subject. This is because we communicate like that. We are not built to understand things perfectly, but we are built to relate to one another.

So become someone that others want to relate to and that you want to be. Doing so will naturally endow you with body language that other people want to be around. Believing in yourself is one of the most comforting things, for yourself, and for everyone else around you. Gaining a sense of confidence cannot be overrated for how much it improves communication.

However, part of learning will always be input. Learn to recognize the body language that you appreciate. There are different philosophies on how to carry yourself and each should be experienced. Go to the gym and learn what the people who obsess over themselves do.

They live to make a potent physical impression, so it seems obvious that they'd have some meaningful lessons for you to pick up on. Every environment has the potential to teach you if you allow it to.

Find the places that you find yourself relaxing. Many people enjoy cafes; others enjoy bars. There's a place for everywhere, whether it's with the mountain folk or in the middle of the city. Find what makes you feel happy to be a part of the conversation and immerse yourself in that culture. Pick up the words that they use, mimic their speed of conversation. Don't imitate them, but try to honestly use the same tools that they use. Over time you will gain a natural inflection with the vocabulary that you have picked up from them. This will allow you to strike a similar profile while you're in conversation so that you can have that body language with you everywhere. Doing so will allow you to contribute what you appreciate wherever you go, and like-minded people will certainly appreciate that.

This is why skater culture exists; they move like one another. After being united by a hobby, they made their own way of speaking, their own gestures, and their own culture. No one owns it, but everyone who dedicates years to it becomes as much of a part of it as anybody else is.

This is how culture works, and the more cultured you are, the better you will hold yourself in situations. Experience is the best teacher.

Live your life being someone that you're interested in being and people will be interested in meeting you.

People with good stories tend to have good conservations, even if they are awkward or wild. Having lived well makes most people sexy.

If you find yourself struggling with the fundamentals, then develop your relationships with the people that trust you. Fighting communities are good, such as boxing gyms. Those communities often have different boundaries than most people are used to, and becoming used to the ways that they physically interact will teach you about what is appropriate.

Physical touch is an important part of communication, and especially body language, but there are many ways it can go wrong.

That's why it's good to start either with fighting communities or with your family.

Both fighting communities and filial communities are environments where you stand to lose nothing by physical interaction.

The boundaries are different in those environments than they are in the rest of the world because bodies are thought of differently.

Dance communities are also a great place to strengthen your understanding of physical boundaries. Any activity that forces physical interaction will make you have to be flexible, and that will teach you better than anything else could.

Otherwise, respect what people communicate and always be willing to give distance.

If something seems to be making someone uncomfortable, then stop doing it.

Doing so will reveal that you have a delicate touch, and this will be appreciated more than the overstepping of the boundary will be remembered in most cases.

It's not about being perfect, but showing finesse and understanding what makes other people comfortable. You don't need to be the smoothest person in the room, but you do need to know how not to be a creep.

Self-care is important in how you present yourself. People will notice the way your shoes look, how you keep your hair if you wear any necklaces, and other such details immediately. Many people don't care about appearances at all, but most do. The way that you present yourself says a lot about the energy that you attract and the lifestyle that you inhabit.

Take time to think about how you present yourself and how you want to present yourself. Some people have a very clean aesthetic and enjoy dressing up in fine clothing. Other people enjoy wearing clothes from thrift stores and jewelry that's meant to enhance the channeling of their chakras.

All of these different philosophies of how to dress reveal a lot about a person's character, and you will tend to get along with people who appreciate the aesthetics that you do.

Authenticity in your life is an important thing, although it is not the only thing.

When it comes to how you dress, how you keep your room, what concerts you go to, and how you eat, though, you should do what you actually want to.

Authenticity can poison conversation, but if you can't be authentic while you're alone, then you're in a bad position.

People can tell when people are appropriating aesthetics, so if you clothe yourself in the styles of other people that you don't appreciate then people will want to avoid you.

Figure out what you enjoy, figure out how to be a part of it, and take care of yourself. All of these will lead you to communicate with great body language, both through posture and tone. Communities teach each other how to talk, that's why the Scottish,

English, Welsh, and Cockney accents exist on the same island, and all of the dialects within those accents. People teach each other ways to recognize each other, and that's how cultures form.

Immerse yourself in one, and you will be included in this process.

Different cultures have different standards. The American public is known not to enjoy touching, while European communities end every conversation with a kiss on the cheek. Religious communities care about how one speaks, and drunkards typical don't trust a man who doesn't curse. There are thousands of different standards for different environments, and subscribing to the ones that you want to be a part of will teach you their ways.

Recognizing the cultures of other people will also make them appreciate you for paying attention to them. Certain tattoos have symbolism behind them. Many people get Japanese characters tattooed, and if you could read the characters on someone, then you would communicate that you were interested in the same thing as them.

It wouldn't matter how you looked, your knowledge on the subject will be a positive enough connection for you

to prove that you're worth interacting with.

In-group and out-group dynamics play a huge role in body language. Negative body language is what people do when they want safety, either from someone they don't know or from a conversation that's headed in a negative direction.

When they feel like they're in the presence of an outsider, they will withhold themselves, closing themselves off from the conversation.

This is because of a basic instinct to mistrust people who you know nothing about, which is an instinct that has kept us alive for thousands of years. Once you can earn their trust, the dynamic will shift to in-group dynamics because they will identify you as one of their own.

This is when their bodies will become more relaxed, and they will become comfortable enough to shift their position or to touch their face.

Mastering body language is the process of mastering how to exist physically as part of a group. By partaking in social activities and deepening the relationships you already have, you will enrichen your understanding of body language, and you will become adept at expressing positively. It's not a theory as much as it's an experience, so make sure that you are a part of the things that you want to be a part of.

❖ Chapter 9 Detecting Specific Personality Traits through Body Language

The functions most responsible for body language are, of course, Si and Se. Ne can also play a large role in how people express themselves. For individuals that rely on Extroverted Intuition, this can be expressed through absurd jokes, such as funny facial expression and physical mischief, like setting a glass on the edge of a table. When paired with Fe this is especially exaggerated.

ENTPs are prone to making absurd jokes that playfully thread the boundaries of what's appropriate.

They like to put people on edge and to push buttons. This is done through sharing slightly private information in public, inside jokes, and playful drawing extreme conclusions from the beliefs of the person they are interacting with.

As for Si and Se, they determine the different styles of body language. Si users tend to belong to a culture, to either their family or a larger unit. Early bonding is how they pick up the standards that end up defining their interactions. If this was not a part of their life, then most often they had to form and adopt standards of their own in the face of whatever adversity plagued them.

In the case of healthy Si users that were allowed the gift of healthy childhoods, their habits will ring through the way that they carry themselves. They will use the words and expression that their loved ones did, and this will be a defining characteristic of how they speak. These archetypes are the true locals who were born with a dialect and will die with it. Their body language tends to be consistent, classic. It's like they inherited stage directions from the older generations. If you're dealing with someone that has static posture and tone taken from the history of wherever they live, then you're most likely dealing with a Si user.

For those that were abandoned or abused, the implementation of Si will be different. Often, instead of carrying the pleasant pieces of those that positively influenced them, those with broken childhoods carry what makes them feel safe. This means that they are often armed with a caustic sense of humor, intimidating postural and gestural habits, and other such jaded features. Once you observe these, then understand what they are and why they exist. Don't take them personally and don't try to change them, instead play along with the games that they do. This is because life taught them that they need to test others to prove that they won't hurt them. Pass their tests out of respect for how difficult life is.

The archetypes that have Si, but are more reliant on Ne, have similar habits to the Si dominants but are still remarkably different. When Ne expresses itself, it expresses itself through novelty, pushing boundaries and conversation to the point that tries to force laughter. Ne users are not prone to relying on the habits of their family because Ne users are often cycling through different habits and new words that they have learned. They're always looking to grow their abilities and their understanding, so although they often express authenticity as their families do, they carry their own posture and other habits.

To tell between Si and Ne dominants notice how much they care. If someone carries themselves like a proud Texan, wearing local brands, and eating meat killed by his buddy, then they probably rely on Si. This is someone who takes their home seriously, is proud to be a part of it, and understands the culture that they come from.

If someone is floaty, changing from week to week while swinging from one idea to the next, but still living with their parents, then they're probably an Ne dominant. They're excellent at chasing potential and changing their habits, but they're still too comfortable with what they were given to truly step out on their own and inherit the responsibility for their lives.

Both of these lifestyles are easy to examine if you know how to pay attention. People who are forgetful think a certain way, and people who never forget anything think a certain way as well. Habits reveal a lot about a person. From whether they dress like their father, or if they are always changing their look, you can usually deduce functions from how others look.

Self-care is also hugely apparent when trying to differentiate between Si and Ne leads. Si users are incredibly in tune with themselves. Due to this, they tend to stay up on bathing, eating, sleeping, cosmetics, and other such things that are meant to take care of their appearance. The mental health of the Si users depends on how well they take care of themselves, which is why most of them end up making sure to give themselves adequate attention. This leads to good posture, slow and confident movements, and good presentation.

Ne users are on the other end of the spectrum. They can be caught sleepless in the middle of public, either ranting to a group of acquaintances about random ideas or working on another project. They are fueled by an incessant quest to bring about something, and this quest can interrupt everything in their life from their eating habits to their bathing habits. They act like they don't even consider their bodies, and thus have wild gestures that don't seem to come from anywhere else but improvisation. If you're talking to someone and it seems like they're not even there, that's likely an Ne dominant.

The Se users are very different in how they end up expressing themselves because it's not directly related to health. ESFPs don't want to be healthy as much as they want to feel good. They're attracted to strength, power, displays of wealth, and otherwise showing themselves off. Life isn't meant to be a humble process of taking care of yourself to them, but a celebration of yourself.

This leads to Se. Loving all things physical, from sports to sports cars, fine dining, and all things powerful. While the Si users enjoy fine cooking, tasting every ingredient used, the Se users love the lighting in the restaurant and the feeling of being out. There's a difference on what's being focused on.

Ironically, Se users tend to have more reserved body language than Si users. This is because Se users are either partaking in explosive action or waiting for it to occur. They know how to hold themselves to look like they belong inside, and how to hold themselves to have fun. They excel at self-control and are able to project incredibly well. Their tastes tend to be more snobbish, and through that, they give off an air of being cultured.

Look out for people who want to set different times for things. If they're running on a schedule, keeping the gym at gym and work at work within the same day without really considering it, then they're probably an Se user. They're using their environments as different stimuli to inspire certain actions from them. Mastering this often reveals a Se dominant.

As for how they carry themselves, posture tends to be important to Se users. While Si users will obsess about their health and take care

of themselves, Se will obsess about what their health means about their value. They will care more about eliminating the dark circles under their eyes than they will care about balancing their schedule so that they have more time to sleep.

Those that rely on Se also tend to be more trusting. They have a pragmatism about them that implies whatever is being talked about is going to be done. Most of them don't enjoy conversations about the future but instead gravitate towards concrete conversations about the near future, such as what can be done within the next two hours. They take things a bit more seriously than Si-Ne users.

The Si-Ne users tend to be the ones who are the most mistrusting. Once they become hurt, they tend never to let go of it and create boundaries that mean it will take weeks to earn their trust. Nothing is accepted at face value by Si-Ne because those who rely on that functional pairing know how easy, and how efficient, it is to lie. It's harder for Se-Ni to imagine doing so because it is more focused on reality than it is on analysis.

So serious body language will be a big indicator of a person's functions. INTJs, ESFPs, ISTPs, and ENFJs all tend to carry themselves very well. They look good in suits, they deliver good speeches, and they are always in the middle of doing something or looking for something to do. These archetypes also tend to have good, appropriate mannerisms. They understand how people are perceived, and they put in the effort to be perceived well.

ENTPs and INTPs will be looking to make people laugh even with they are giving the most important speeches in their careers. ESFJs and ISFJs are much the same way, always wanting peace while loving incredibly biting jokes.

These archetypes take themselves much less seriously than the Se-Ni archetypes do. This is because Si-Ne sees that there is a history that exists, and there is a future that will exist. Due to this knowledge, most of the users of Si-Ne are at peace with knowing that anything that needs to happen will most likely happen, and if they want something to happen, it's merely a matter of putting in the effort.

For Se-Ni users the experience of living is much more personal. They perceive the world around them for its sensory features but also are subject to an incredible and unexplainable vision. This vision tunes them into something that they think is important, either an essential truth or a prophecy, and it is that which motivates them to partake in the world around them. This philosophy has much more gravitas than the philosophy of those who see that life existed before them and that it will exist long after them.

The difference is that Si-Ne assumes that everything is a potential reality. This means that anything could happen, that all goals are achievable, and all things are possible. If you want something, then you merely need to manifest the energy required to bring it into existence. They see life as a creative process that has more to do with random chance than it has to do with true control, and so they live their lives trying to play to the whims of fate and to take advantage of what already existed long before they did.

Those that use Se-Ni see life as a personal journey. They don't tend to think of themselves as one more in an infinite line of humans; they feel themselves as the force that they are. Often they believe in their own uniqueness and that they can truly have an impact on the world around them. Instead of thinking this arises out of luck, Se-Ni users see it as the product of work. This means that when they want to

accomplish something they set out to do so seriously, and they build each part systematically.

These differences in philosophy make for wildly different habits. Si- Ne users tend to chat endlessly about nothing, enjoying working up to absurd premises that mean nothing, and pondering questions that can never be answered. To them there is no wasted time, time passes no matter what you do. This allows them to take on the character of the jester, and to live life with a loose grip. Se-Ni users feel the opposite, that all time spent on ineffable questions is wasted time, and that goals should be worked towards. They want life to be meaningful, and so they design their lives to contain things that they consider meaningful, such as prayer and meditation.

Read these energies in the people that you interact with. If they're jumping from one subject to the other, speaking with their hands, and unkempt, then they are most likely an Ne dominant. If the person you're speaking to is incredibly measured, well researched in their interests, and carries themselves with respectable poise, then they are most likely an archetype that relies on Se-Ni.

❖ Chapter 10 Detecting Lies

This theory is very prone to be abused by manipulators because it allows for an impressive amount of insight into the way that different people are cognizant of the worldaround them.

This information easily allows individuals with twisted interests to take advantage of what is inherently a part of some people, using their strengths and habits to trap them into performing whatever actions they would like to convince them to partake in. When considering this, it's important both to know the strengths of the people out there who want to manipulate you and to know your own weaknesses.

Manipulators have a great front. They project a confident, extroverted energy which feels like you should believe they are a trustworthy person. When you are exposed to this energy, the feeling is subtle.

Decades of the manipulators' lives have been spent refining their strategy so that they could strike the right impression on their targets.

If you have any sort of insecurity or inability to supply yourself with what you desire, then you are the ideal target for these sorts of people. Any instability within yourself can be played against you to great effect. This is because if you don't have complete confidence within yourself, then you are more prone to believing someone else's attempt to convince you that you need help, or that they know better.

So, one of the first things to develop to protect yourself will be to become in tune with your emotional energies. Realize what parts of yourself are being spoken to when you're in a conversation, and take notice of anything being played.

There are several attributes that can be played against someone, so notice if there are any weak spots within yourself.

For example, if someone is insecure about their ability to navigate, then they might follow the same path every day due to the suggestion of someone that they met outside. This path just happens to coincide with the place where the person who gives the direction hangs out every day. Through suggesting this path, that person now has an opportunity on a daily basis to both ask for favors, and to work on planting more seeds of thoughts in their target's head.

It's hard to notice this behavior because manipulative people get good over time. If they didn't then, they would be run out of town by a mob wielding pitchforks, but it is through their social graces that they often end up in comfortable places within our societies.

This is what makes them so dangerous; they can be found anywhere you would find anyone else. They are masters of camouflage.

This is why the body must be consulted. We don't feel good when we are being controlled, in fact, we develop brain fog, we have less motivation to accomplish the things we were interested in, and general pains set in. All of these symptoms can appear when you are the target of a manipulator, and often many of them will. If they do, don't blame yourself. Consider how you are being treated and see if there are any relationships in your life that you need to address. Often we are too afraid to question the people in our life to admit that we are being wronged. Give yourself the permission to be the victim, and analyze your relationships in as unbiased a way as you can possibly manage.

Addressing your own proclivity towards being manipulated is the most important step in defending against dark energy because you

need to be aware of how you can be played. Once you know your vulnerabilities and how it feels when they are preyed upon, then you will be able to recognize when someone is manipulating you. This is the first step in protecting yourself from that and reversing whatever they are attempting to do. If you cannot do this, then you will not be able to defend yourself from manipulative people adequately. They know how to bend people better than you understand how people should look, so the best strategy for you to adopt is to know yourself as best as you can, there is no way that they've been able to learn to understand you as much as you understand yourself.

Once you have achieved protecting yourself, then you can focus on the different sorts of lies. Every individual has their own style, there are as many ways to lie as there are waves in the sea, but there are still certain habits that liars tend to have. The easiest way to break them up is into the extroverted functions, but the introverted functions play a large role in lying as well.

Extroverted Intuition is the perhaps the best friend of the manipulator. It allows people the insight, understanding, and finesse necessary to pick up information on their target, understand how their target relates to that information, and how to play it against them. The way to recognize the presence of manipulative Ne is that you feel like your thoughts are being completed, but you're not finishing them. You're vocalizing yourself, but your sentences are almost being finished for you, the other person in the conversation is following what you say to conclusions that make a lot of sense, but weren't quite what you were thinking of.

This style of manipulation is incredibly effective, and difficult to perceive because it imitates a normal conversation almost perfectly. They develop the conversation as if they're incredibly interested, asking pertinent questions and trying to contribute to your ideas, but they're doing so to earn your trust, not to engage with you.

You can feel this by realizing that you're not expressing yourself, but being herded along to wherever the other person is taking you.

Extroverted Feeling is another function with excellent use as a manipulative tool, although Fe is best utilized by women. This is because society is built around women using Fe as their form of communication and expression. Due to this many women, and men, have used their decades of experience with the function to warp it into a way to drive others. It works through applying social pressure.

The way that Extroverted Feeling works are that the pressures from the atmosphere of the environment or the conversation influences the moods of those who use it. Those with a dark interest in Fe take advantage of that to gain whatever they want by manipulating these moods. One of the easiest examples is using relationship standards to either drain a significant other for resources, or to convince them to change, or both. This is so effective because Fe leads are some of the most charming people within our society; again, it was built for them.

To notice the influence of this form of manipulation you only need to look at your self-image. Being manipulated like this absolutely destroys how you think about yourself, and how you think of your place within the world. If your confidence is absolutely abhorrent while everyone else is convincing you that you're fine, that you're doing a great job and that you belong where you do, then run. People who care about you don't try to convince you nothing is wrong when you feel awful. They respect your feelings and listen to you. They don't want you to feel the negative emotions that you do, but they respect your right to and offer any sort of support that they can. If that's not what happens with the situation you're in, then you're likely under the influence of toxic Fe users.

Extroverted Thinking is a favorite tool of the narcissists. Through it, they can validate all of their egoism and caustic thinking. Science, religion, culture, and academia all become mere material for them to use to spin to prove their points. They will use any sort of authority to claim the right to lord over the people in their lives, using their access to knowledge as proof of their superiority. This is one of the most effective manipulative tactics not because it's hard to recognize, or because it's sustainable, but because narcissists are incredibly brazen people. Even if they're causing terrible harm to the people around them, they are likely to stay their course and remain uncaring about the effects of their beliefs and statements.

Finally, Extroverted Sensation is the tool of those who want to distract. They use their abilities to sense space and to create a good atmosphere to lure people into a certain mindset. Often this is done to build trust with their target, or to lead their target away from a trail which would reveal the misdoings of the manipulator. To convince their targets they make use of food, sex, aesthetics, comfort, and any of the other bodily comforts to distract them while the manipulator pursues their true goal. This is easy to observe due to the literal evidence that this tactic often leaves behind. If someone is treating you to great things while making you feel terrible, then this is probably the tactic that they are using.

There are many other ways to manipulate, and all of the introverted functions have their nuances, but the extroverted functions are easier to examine performing this activity. Still, don't study these as definitions, but outlines, or sketches. Apply this knowledge to your own life as a way to try to organize your experience, but not to define it. Define your life for yourself, and you will be safe.

❖ Chapter 11 Incompatibility

There are many myths concerning the incompatibility between types. Ultimately, the only truth is that maturity rises above everything and that every archetype can get along with every other archetype. With understanding, all miscommunication and difference can be worked past. Some types have an easier time communicating with one another, but there are no two types that cannot get along.

To claim that there are is to misunderstand the theory, for the archetypes do not define people, but people define the archetypes.

It is commonly understood that opposites work well together, and so there are few theories that claim that types such as the ISTJ and ENFPs cannot form meaningful relationships. Most people who study the theory understand the relationship between ISTJs and ENFPs are actually incredibly fertile and can lead to balance within the lives of both of the types.

Starting from there, we can understand that even the archetypes that are diametrically opposed are widely compatible.

After those pairings, the next one that could be argued would be those that have entirely different functions. As discussed before, an example of this relationship would be between the ENTJs and the INTPs. While the ENTJs have Te-Ni-Se-Fi INTPs have Ti-Ne-Si-Fe, so they are completely mismatched in terms of function. This doesn't mean anything about the compatibility of these types, however.

First, everyone develops uniquely. It is generally true the INTPs rely on Ti-Ne to work on unorthodox theories, and that they are excited to work on projects that allow them to work on new problems. Some INTPs completely buck this profile though and actually train themselves in Te to better communicate their ideas publically. These INTPs value community over their own inherent tendencies, and so they are versed in scientific literature, and other such sources of authority.

These INTPs can get along incredibly well with ENTJs because they know how to communicate in a way that is complementary to the ENTJ archetype.

Alternatively, many ENTJs want to explore the blind spots of human knowledge. Although they are very able to pick up scientific knowledge, and other such systemized information, easily, some of them still feel a need to expand into the knowledge that isn't as proven. These ENTJs can develop their sense for Ti and grow a respect for people who think in ways that others are too afraid too, which makes them incredibly able to communicate with INTPs.

No type of limits who you can interact with and your life will do much more to supply you with your preferences than your archetype will. Positive experiences with the various archetypes throughout your life will do more to determine your compatibility with other archetypes than your functions.

This has dipped into discussing shadow functions, as the primary shadow functions for ENTJs is Ti and the primary shadow function for INTPs is Te. The existence of the shadow functions is important because everyone has every single function. Everyone is capable of communicating in all of the different ways that humans communicate; it simply takes maturity and patience for them to arrive at a point where they can have nothing but good conversations.

Second, the functions don't need to be perfectly aligned for communication. ISFPs and ISTPs can make for great friends even though their views of the world are nearly opposite.

Peopleappreciate variety, and both archetypes have a unique perspective to share with the other. This is what matters. Any sort of mathematical formula that predicts how people get along will be wildly inaccurate.

The different pairings are harmonious in their own ways. Ti-Fe pairs well with Te-Fi because the different individuals can represent all of the different reactions to stimuli. As the Fe-Ti user is trying to figure out the reasons that agreed upon things are valued, the Te-Fi user can offer up an explanation that is based both in society's beliefs and their own interpretation.

This provides the grounds for a pregnant conversation, as the diversity of viewpoints can lead the conversation anywhere. There is no disadvantage if the individuals make sure to tend to their weaknesses and not force their opinions.

As you open yourself up to the different relationships that can form, you will become better at dealing with everybody. The more experience that you have with dealing with diversity, the better you will be at dealing with people in general. This is why thinking about incompatibility is so ill-advised. If you close yourself off to dynamics because you believe they won't be healthy or valid, then those relationships have no opportunity to flourish. It is possible to kill things before they had a chance to sprout.

So keep an open mind, and anyone can be a friend. You are not limited by yourself or by other people. The more flexible you become, the more others will be flexible for you. If you don't insist on getting your way, all dynamics will become much easier to deal with. The willingness that you show to understand others will be returned.

These archetypes have existed for thousands of years, at least in theory. Human society has had to adapt to the fact that people are different from each other forever, and we have made it for millennia

getting along just fine. No one had to be sacrificed and kicked off the boat to make room; everybody gets to stay.

Consider this while you interact with others. Our history proves that we are abler to get along than we are prone to destroy each other. Humans listen to each other, especially as they grow older. Showing finesse and dealing with people by being able to interact with everyone will show that you understand this history. People are not valuable for their personalities, but for themselves. We are all worth living because we have life. There is no one who is undeserving, and so we all deserve respect, no matter how differently we think. As you become capable of following people who think differently than you, you will become wiser. Sages don't pick who approaches them, but they make themselves available. Be like a sage. Welcome whatever energy stumbles into your life.

When you are particularly put off by a certain archetype, you should examine your history. If you had an abusive father, then you will either be prone to hate his archetype or to attract it into your life. This is more often the root of communication issues than any sort of functional compatibility. We are the sum of our experiences. Don't assume that a certain type of people is good or bad just because you feel a certain way about them.

Instead, you should examine the root of that feeling. If it stems from abuse, then work to get past that abuse and let go of the energy it left you with. When you assume that someone is abusive, you often make an abuser out of them. Our thoughts manifest into our lives, so exercise caution in your prejudices.

If your family life was poor as a child then either reform a social unit or do what you can to address your relationship with your loved ones. Address the insecurities and tensions that have grown over time, and try to do so honestly. If you feel like your father never listens to you, then tell him that. If he gets angry at you, then find someone else to talk to.

So many of our issues with other people are actually issues we have with ourselves. This is why it's important to learn to express well. Your frustrations with other people might actually be due to your inability to reach them, not anything about them. Understand this before you claim that you can't get along with any group of people. There is probably unresolved trauma if you feel that way, and that issue you can address. Doing so will benefit you both with peace of mind, and the ability to better communicate with those that are around you.

Addressing these issues takes years for many people, but it is the true cause of not being able to get along with others. If every ESTJ you meet fights with you then you're probably out looking to fight with ESTJs. You probably don't think you are if you suffer from this, but it's much more likely than you being incompatible with that type. People who leave us with pain poison our ability to interact with others for the rest of our lives. Don't let them win. Let go of whatever they left you with and embrace humanity. It is your true family.

If you cannot identify any trauma that gives you a distaste for a certain group of people, then look at your maturity level. It may be the case that you don't know how to express yourself in different ways, and so you aren't able to express yourself adequately to certain archetypes. If this is happening, then you simply need to work on yourself and gain experience communicating with people who are different then you. Keep the fact that different people think

differently in mind, and try to communicate with others in a way that they will appreciate.

Once you can read people well, then you can manipulate them. That is the dark truth to this theory. Understanding people does give you an advantage over them, and it allows you to act in ways that they don't understand.

This can be misused to a disgusting degree, and you can truly harm the people that you target, but it can also be a way to work past someone you have difficulties with.

What you shouldn't do is target an INFP, realize their habits, and then become a consistent and honest influence in their life just to earn their trust. Doing things like that is creepy because you're taking advantage of habits that the INFP might be unaware of even having. It's easy to target the sentimentality and their need to express themselves, but don't do so if you have no honest intention of building a relationship with you. Karma is not kind to those who take advantage of others.

You can freely manipulate yourself, however. If you recognize that you're dealing with an INFP while you're an ISTP, then you can shift how you act to communicate with them. Don't do things that will miscommunicate your character, but allow more space in conversation. They will want to talk about things in personal and emotional terms. Allow them to do so and listen to what they're expressing. Ask questions instead of giving advice, and spend most of the conversation listening. If you are patient and understanding, then you will contribute more than enough to the conversation for them to feel like you had a great interaction. Doing this will also teach you how they process information, and you will respect it more after you observe it. It's hard to understand why people are the way they are until you see how it works for them.

Keep loose and fluid. By working with their attributes instead of your own, you start the conversation with a major advantage. It's when you feel the need to force your perspective that conversations go sour. Resistance only exists if you contribute to it.

Don't let yourself be fooled; you can be friends with anybody if you're open to it. There are no incompatibilities. Maturity serves as the attribute that can unite all people, no matter where they're from or how they act. Be patient, listen well, and don't force yourself. Acting this way will let you get along with everybody.

Be honest if you carry any trauma with you, and be honest if it clouds your judgment. If it does, then work with it and learn not to judge people before they reveal themselves to you. If all goes well, one day you will be able to let go of the trauma and be free to live your life as you deserve to. Until then, don't let your mind make people up. Let people prove who they are. Listen to action, not prejudice.

❖ Chapter 12 Listening to Hear

he ability to listen is an underrated attribute which is losing traction in the modern era. As we continually refine our technology information is placed on a higher and higher pedestal. This results in people being crushed by their own anxiety to speak correctly. They spend too much energy on considering what they're going to say. Their brains are too taxed to listen, so they lose out on the opportunity to communicate because they don't have the energy.

If you want to communicate with anybody, then focus on your ability to listen. This is the ruling principle in good conversation. People who aren't capable of understanding what the other person they're talking to is saying are incapable of meaningful conversation. Your archetype doesn't matter in terms of limiting your ability to communicate, your maturity and your patience do.

There is more in the world than you can imagine. Your thoughts will never assist you in maintaining a conversation if you retreat into them. Developing your ability to be present is paramount to good communication.

Functions are relatively unimportant when considering how to communicate with others, but it may be helpful to focus on your extroverted energies. By addressing how you relate to the world through your functions, you can find pathways that are easier for you personally. Focus on whatever energy feels natural for you to partake in conversation as long as it is successful.

You'll need to balance yourself well to become a good listener, whether or you're introverted or extroverted. Even extroverts tend to be poor listeners, so don't assume that a social presence is the same thing as emotional depth. Instead, think about the conversations that you're having as you have them.

Asking questions you honestly have is a great place to start. By asking questions during the conversations, you partake in you will communicate that you are actively participating in it. No one wants to feel like they're talking without being understood, so by interacting with what they have said you will show that you're trying your best to understand them. Ultimately, that's the best that we can do.

There is no perfect understanding that you can achieve; every conversation will have some thoughts left unexplained. This is because we cannot harness telepathy at will, we have to rely on context clues and tone to figure out what other people mean. Realize this and humble yourself. Get used to the fact that there will always be more for you to learn than you know.

Addressing the way that pride is a part of your life and focusing on the present is the only way to start actually listening to the people around you. Most people don't even do that, so starting to better your abilities as a communicator will place you in a far better position than most. It's not that hard to develop yourself, but many are too selfish even to sacrifice the time.

However, once you go against the common ways, you will realize how rich communication actually can be. Listening allows you the opportunity to be an active part of the conversation. Instead of having to imagine the right thing to say, or decoding the principle of people's thoughts in your heads, you can simply get rid of having to do any of that by being present.

People want to communicate. No conversations are intended to be useless, so if you work with someone to understand what they want to express, then everything will go smoothly. Things are supposed to work out, and a little bit of effort can change everything. Even saying less in conversation so that people have the room to flesh out their positions fully can radically improve your conversations.

There's no value in being a doormat, of course. Active listening doesn't mean completely retreating from your own rights to expression. If someone is continually talking at you then make sure to interject into their stream of consciousness, or else they may forget that you are even there. This is another reason why asking questions is a great strategy because it proves that you are to be addressed, not talked at.

If someone responds to questions like you're not there, then they're awful communicators. It's never the case that everything is your fault, so always be ready to consider the different factors that go into a conversation. If you've tried everything that you can and interacting with someone makes you feel awful no matter what, then disengage from the situation.

The way that people reply to questions speaks volumes about their personalities. If they seriously consider them and then take the time out of the diatribe to contemplate their answers, then there's a lot of hope for great conversation with them. It's a sign of good culture to be able to help people understand what you're discussing, even if the person you're talking to has no experience with what you're talking about. This is because it shows that you're interested in communicating ideas no matter who you are speaking to, rather than someone obsessively following a train of thought. No one enjoys

being talked at, so by working to treat people with respect and patience, you'll avoid coming across as mean.

Meanness is perhaps the worst attribute to have, no matter what kind of person you are. People are sensitive, and they are quick to withdraw when they feel offended or undervalued. One of the worst ways to offend someone is to communicate that you're not listening as they speak. Developing your ability to be attentive and to respond to the conversational cues that come up is a safe strategy to avoid this.

We all carry the responsibility to listen. There are no listeners and talkers, but humans, and to communicate a human must go through the entire range of expression. Don't cut people slack for the way that they are, or because of your relationship to them, and don't let yourself get away with things that you shouldn't.

Understand that the responsibility falls squarely on our own shoulders and that we must have the conversations and relationships that we wish to see in the world. All of us get to decide what reality is and will be through our action. Make sure to use your input wisely.

We are taught how to listen through our environments and the people we are surrounded by. Most people who struggle to communicate, both in listening and speaking, were abused in some way. This is because we remember how we are treated, and the standards that are set in childhood are often the standards that we carry with us throughout life. If you react with impatience or distaste to someone who doesn't know how to socialize properly, then you will only be reaffirming this processing of the world.

Try to break the cycle by giving them a different standard to work with. Support what they say, communicate with positive energy and

healthy posture and generally be a good friend. Tell them that you're there for them and promise that you're not going away. Many people have to have this amount of support to feel comfortable to begin expressing themselves. Demonstrate a different way of treating others than they have known and you will often be rewarded with a great friend.

If they respond to this only by recreating the dynamics from their trauma, then there is nothing that you can do. Some issues can only be addressed by the self, or by doctors. It is better to have tried and been wrong than it is to be a coward. Don't feel like you have to save anybody that you have given your attention, talking to someone isn't an agreement that you'll be the cure to their issues. Give them your best effort, listen to them, and be caring, but if that doesn't work then head out on your own way. Life is too fragile to let people who want to tear you down hang around. Respect your own space and health, too. Learning how to listen also means learning to listen to yourself.

Being able to disengage from toxic behavior is one of the best attributes that someone can have if they want to be a positive influence in general.

The kindest people are the people who are most commonly preyed upon by serial killers. This speaks to a reality that evil does not want a fair fight; it wants to stalk and defile what is better than it. Learn how to work around this by being kind, but kind with a backbone. Give as much as you want, but never let people take from you. Force people to get permission before any of your resources are used.

There are thousands of ways that people can try to communicate with you to manipulate you into doing something for them. It's difficult to be wise to all of them, but luckily, humans were gifted with an amazing gut. No matter how good someone is at lying, your body will know when you are being lied to. Our gut processes our feelings as much as our brain or our heart, so be aware when you feel uncomfortable. Often it is because you are correctly divining something about the situation.

So, respect that.

Once you start to feel unwell around someone, or your spirits sink when you have to interact with them, then disassociate. It is great to listen to people who are different than you, and we must keep open minds, but never let someone into your life that disrupts your natural energy.

Living in alignment takes balancing several aspects of your life until you can truly inhabit yourself and your environment. If there are people in your life that expose both to negative energies, then the journey to find harmony will become that much harder.

Some of us are blessed with good families, and if you are then tend to yours. A family is a holy unit, which has within itself the map for our psyche to use while we enter into the world and navigate communicating with the 8 billion other people in our species.

A good relationship with your family, especially your parents, will deeply ground you and teach you about interacting with people that are different than yourself.

Listening used to be the most important skill. Before we had cities, before we had homes, we still had to communicate. Seasons changed, wars were fought, diseases ravaged populations, and farming had to be invented. All of these things could only be addressed by thousands of people communicating, and communicating well. It was through our association with one another that the modern era was born.

Nowadays we don't have to worry about those issues, as they have been handled, but now we've lost out on the necessity and the utility of clear expression. This is why the family can be so helpful. It is a holdover from the time of the tribes, as we needed families to survive and to bring up the future generations. The inherent structure behind it still has a piece of those wild societies that we first formed, back where communication wasn't an option but the norm.

Working with conversation, listening, and expression and in general in terms of the utility of them is the best approach.

We are creatures that are meant to express, not necessarily to think. For thousands of years, we got along without written language, so you shouldn't have to strain yourself too hard to be able to carry a good conversation.

If you're anxious about conversation, or you still don't know how to approach it, then bring in that prehistoric atmosphere.

Don't address people for the schools that they've attended, or for the ways that they compartmentalize modern living, but address them for what they are – for what we all are – flesh with consciousness. Get along with prime apes, and you'll be able to get along with anybody.

❖ Conclusion

There's much to gain from being able to read others, but make sure you use this ability responsibly. It's very easy to hurt others, so make sure you're doing your best to be a good influence, not merely an active one. The understanding that you have gained about human psychology is very powerful knowledge, and I encourage everybody to exercise caution as they try to implement what they have learned.

Still, the majority of this journey will be a personal one. The more that you understand about yourself, the more you will be able to understand others. Invest in your relationship with yourself, respect yourself, and take care to listen to yourself. You will show yourself what it means to be human.

We all work from this position, and we're all more similar than we are different. Embrace your fellow person and don't be afraid to resemble them.

Don't think that you're special, or than anybody else is. We are all animals, and we all want to have good lives.

Remember to be humble. People appreciate people who know how challenging life is, and so showing that you don't suffer from your self-image will show that you know how to live. No one knows everything, and no one has to. All you need to be is the best you that you can be, and to listen well.

If any of this information was useful to you, then a review on Amazon would be deeply appreciated. There are many resources available to learn about Yung's theories. However, most prefer to discuss pop psychology rather than the theory. If you appreciate how technical this book was, then please stand by it with a review. Thank you for your time, and I wish you well.

www.ingramcontent.com/pod-product-compliance
Lightning Source LLC
LaVergne TN
LVHW022003060526
838200LV00003B/73